Insight Without Change Is Meaningless

byOrtheä Bäker Gätes

Copyright © 2021 by Dorotheä Bäker Gätes
All rights reserved
First Edition

PAGE PUBLISHING, INC.
Conneaut Lake, PA

First originally published by Page Publishing 2021

ISBN 978-1-64544-820-4 (pbk)
ISBN 978-1-64544-821-1 (digital)

Printed in the United States of America

"As Dorothea Gates' lifelong friend and assistant, it has been a real pleasure to assist her and her many clients. The feedback received from so many of them that she has helped, including my family, is truly amazing! Many ask, "How does she know these things about me and my life when I've told no one before?" My answer is that God, the Creator, has blessed Dorothea with this beautiful Divine gift. She is successful in her ability to help on such a grand scale because, as a prophet, she uses the blessed gift the way that God wants her to use it. This journey has been spectacular so far and I look forward to the adventures yet to come.

My name is Lucille Shannon and as a registered Reflexologist and a former owner of Shannon Reflexology Center/Buckhead Wellness Center, I am exposed and knowledgeable about practitioners of healing and those who have gifts."

"Dorothea has literally saved my life on many occasions from counseling me not to take my life or the life of others. Giving grief counseling when I lost my best friend and baby sister. Her guidance has always been a white light in my life. Anytime she gives me a reading it is always on point and has been that way for 30 years. She is a true gift on this earth and the universe."

-Evelyn Mims
WXIA Affiliate (ret)

Erica Wright, CEO and Founder of U First Inc. A 501 (c)(3) nonprofit organization based in Atlanta, Georgia. Our mission is to provide the essential hygiene items for our friends experiencing homelessness around the world. As a Master Barber for over 35 plus years I found myself on a spiritual journey to find myself through my brokenness and depression. But to my surprise I found my passion in serving.

While seeking advice and knowledge I was introduced to Dorothea 12 years ago through a close friend to seek advice. Little did I know Dorothea would be a powerful force in my healing and finding my voice, the true power of prayer in gratitude and forgiveness. Our conversation reached beyond the journey of a selfless friendship. Dorothea insight to healing communities gave us an unbreakable bond. Learning the word love through Dorothea's eyes is contagious. Her words to live life to the fullest is empowering and uplifting.

I am truly excited to see the words to paper as Dorothea has help to shape and reshape the journey of so many who have crossed her path. When I think of the butterfly I often think of Dorothea, knowing her personal journey of unrest for people to thrive, to be well within will metamorphosis into this book. Dorothea would always say "transformation, starts within" so I pray you find your internal voice as you flip the pages of this book. Allowing Dorothea's voice to leap from the pages on your personal journey that will take you from past hurt, trauma and pain to healing and being who God created you to be.

Ms. Erica Wright, CEO and Founder of U First, Inc.
Board Member for Gatway Center in Atlanta
Out Georgia Business Alliance Ambassador

Acknowledgments

I would like to thank my children, Travis and Talia, for their wonderful patience with their mother. I would like to thank Cathy Mathis for her wonderful patience and her diligence in always believing in me.

I would like to wholeheartedly thank a very special person who, without her, this book might not be in existence. She pushed and pushed for me to get this book out and proofread the first draft. Thank you, Deborah Young-Salter, for your wonderful friendship.

In addition to proofreading the final draft, to my wonderful long-term mentor, friend, mom, and assistant, Lucille Shannon, thank you for helping me when I felt so alone.

I would like to thank my graphics team Sharlise Lowe at Graphics by Sax. Thank you for my book cover, your diligence, know-how, and creativity—you are always appreciated.

I would also like to thank Evelyn Mims, Porsche Foxx, Joyce Littel, Carol Blackmon, Silas Si-Man Baby Alexander, Derek Harper, Kwasi McCoy, and a host of radio and TV personalities that gave me my start.

The Game of Love and How to Play It
Conversations with a Metaphysician

The Question-and-Answer Series

I would like to take you to another place to capture the transactional flow of life. A portrait is presented to us through social media, advertisement, promotional and campaign ads on how family-friendly gatherings should be demonstrated to the society. Do you think love and relationships are big businesses that express the interaction of mankind? The advertisement market sets the stage on how we interact with each other. Let's move forward so that I can tell you how life is woven together to generate a feeling.

Life presents various twists and turns; however, the standard theme among humans is the innate desire to be loved, respected, and understood. Imagine the glimpses of happiness presented to us daily: two-parent homes or, in some cases, single-parent homes with well-behaved children. Almost everywhere one can look up and find various types of visuals displayed on campaign ads, billboards, dental, amusement parks, realty, plumbing, grocery stores, and the number one visual being family-friendly ads are restaurants.

The most persuasive billboard is the nightlife billboard, which often contains alcohol and women. You will find on these billboards: sexy women, women that exemplify a relaxing environment dancing in front of handsome men. Next there are the cigarette ads that display images of the happy smoker. It is inviting to see a smoker gathered in a crowd with a cigarette between their fingers; enjoying the pleasure of smoking in a catchy promotional display on cigarettes. Another successful cigarette ad is displayed with a person with a smile on their face, entering a flashy car with a cigarette in one hand. These are just a few subtle glimpses of the good life as depicted by the billboard philosophy.

Not only does the billboard replicate an ideal of happiness; the holiday seasons also present its own glimpses of happiness and joy. Personally, I enjoy Thanksgiving, which I have affectionately termed "Gratitude Day." I enjoy watching family-friendly television, commercials depicting love and joy while simultaneously creating wonderful holiday memories. Families harmoniously gather around the holiday dinner table trimmed with smiles and all the fixings.

There are a lot of commercials on television that remind us of love, giving, and forgiveness. These advertisements are a constant reminder of how touching and poignant, starting from Halloween to Christmas, commercials and advertisements are—a reminder of love, giving, and forgiveness, which can be very touching and emotional. The skillful advertiser captures the climate of its investors and occasionally hits below the seasonal pocket, as well as sentimental heartstrings during the holiday seasons.

All these examples of joy, love, happiness, and forgiveness are expressions that are advertised in cards. Hallmark is running the show when airing its emotionally charged commercials, reminding people that it's always going to be okay if you take the attention off yourself and give it to someone who needs an outpouring of love. Night after night the Hallmark channel gives us warm, wonderful feelings of hope for a wonderful future. For instance, Christmas commercials depicting Rudolph and Santa on the roof of a beautifully lit home while the children gaze out of the window in anticipation. There is also the image of the husband surprising the wife with a large diamond ring or a vehicle wrapped in bows sitting in the driveway, and lastly, the prodigal son returning home for a holiday feast with family.

There are those commercials that give us the impression of what romance and happy families look like. These illustrations depict notions of fatherhood and make becoming a new mother appear so sweet and ultrafeminine. It's a lifelike Rockwell's painting. In years past, Rockwell, the artist, painted happy family scenes of what America can and should be. Looking at these examples, one might say, "Ahh, that's how my life should be." A loving man coming home with flowers that he's holding behind his back and kissing the woman ever so passionately as he walks her outside the front door, where there is a car wrapped in ribbon as a surprise just for being the best gift in his life.

Love songs of every genre put you in a romantic mood of the promise of hope and forever after with endless nights of love and passion. The promise and hope are big deals, so are to be loved and coupled in many days, nights, and years of mutual love, respect, and understanding. That's what I see when I see these commercials of touching and poignant attentiveness; it gets to me all the time. Imagine the effect it has on a hopeless romantic that can eat and sleep romance twenty-four hours a day. Romance can be sweet, touching, thoughtful, and attentive. The flipside can look like needy, claustrophobic, smothering, stalking, and obsessive love, which is the opposite of a healthy romance. It is unhealthy insecurities in which some form of counseling should be investigated to facilitate and alleviate this compulsion. The relationships we attract reflect who we are and what we think we want; it comes what we invite in our lives. Whatever we spot in our relationships, whether it is positive or negative, we are a remnant of that which we see.

What type of relationships are you attracting into your life? Love, intimate, platonic, family, work, public… How are you maintaining these relationships? What beliefs do you carry that contribute to the growth of relationships all around you and that you are in? Do you believe it's just animal attraction, the luck of the dice, kismet, or just allowing nature to take its course? Do you think that you can have the person of your desires, or do you believe that whatever comes in, you are stuck with it? All that is true if you think it, so for those of you that believe that, fine. For others who believe relationships are a mirror of who we are and the beliefs that are in us, that is true as well. Relationship thoughts compile a mile high on how far we must go to improve upon ourselves to be happy and attract what we truly deserve. Our relationships are our teachers, and we are the students, in addition to being lovers, friends, partners, and beneficiaries. Relationships stand to teach us a great deal, and there is much in store for those who are willing participants in the game of love.

Paradigm shifts…wouldn't it be nice if synchronicity of events could take place in your life, and a soul-mate love appears (*poof*), pops in on the scene, thus taking out the work in seeking a suitable life mate that meets your criteria? *Wham.* Abracadabra, it would all be taken care of. Bim, bam, *poof,* it is done! It is interesting that the phrase "meeting our every need" is so popular instead of being the best you can be to attract the best in someone else.

The idea of having a relationship is, in many ways, a feeling of completion for most people. In my practice, I delve into the topic of relationships about 95 percent of the time; this is the most prolific part of what I do. The questions an individual may have in their session with me vary; some may not want the session to be about relationships, so they focus on other items such as work or family. However, when a relationship question is posed, impassioned words and gestures start to come out.

These questions may be any of the following: Will I be alone for the rest of my life or at least this year? Is he or she the one for me? What are their thoughts about me? What is the future like for the two of us? Is he or she marriage material? Is he or she involved with anyone else, and if so, how can I be the main feature in his or her life, as the best candidate? How long has this person been in their life, and are they leaving soon? When is he getting a divorce? When will the divorce be final? Am I pregnant? I want to know because I'm too scared to get a pregnancy test, and will he be happy about it? How can I get him? What is the best way to make the most out of this relationship? How much money does he make? I don't know what he does for a living. Does he have a job? How much money does he make, will he be able to support me? How long will we last? Is he or she cheating? Is he gay? Something must be wrong with her; is she lesbian?

Now, these are a few of the real questions I receive daily, and these are the questions I get asked far more often than asking about the individual's finances and career. Now, do not get me wrong, career and finances are a very close second to be asked about if time permits. So I say to you, love is the most powerful force known to mankind that allows a person to feel invincible, giving the comfort of feeling safe and secure with thoughts of lifelong satisfaction.

Talking with thousands of people over years has shown me that we all have a desire to be loved. It does not matter what about your status or education level is in life. Love is all-encompassing, and its power can lift anyone of us out of the doldrums to happy wholeness. To be honest, no one wants to be alone for the rest of their life, but the need for lots of me-time or space for themselves could be a turnoff for those who want to often be close to their partner. You do not want to be penalized for taking this amount of space.

Many times an individual is penalized because of the stigma created when one partner feels complete by being in the company of their lover all the time outside work. With this stigma, insecurities begin to creep in depending on the baggage of the person who wants to spend as much time with their selected partner as possible. Sliding in comes the downward spiral of discontent and delusion, which creates havoc in one's mind, setting up a continual stage of rejection, fueling the fire of what is already in the belief system of the needy partner. Now it goes from creating that warm enduring relationship to the negative connotations coming up, and ultimately, the partner with the need for space creating a space of aloneness instead of visualizing a partner that really meets their needs despite if they've never seen it or even think it exists; they visualize it anyway.

The most wonderful thing about being in a relationship is knowing that you will not be alone. The most natural dream is to meet, fall in love, and live happily ever after; so we think, so we hope, so we believe, so we want. In all actuality, life is full of love detours that not only bring in difficulty but also bring what are we full of in the inside. This is what we are attracting, but why is really the question.

There are many ways to interpret relationships. We must keep in mind that relationships correlate to an individual's specific life pattern; a combination of details tells the tale of what is brought in to our so-called love relationships. Relationships are about coming together and ultimately not being alone. It can be argued that a wedding is a dream for most women—

whether it be walking down the aisle to the altar or traveling to a destination. Before the goal can be realized, you must find someone you can build a life with.

Building a life is all-encompassing and may include sharing thoughts, interest, similarities, attraction, and/or scents. These things will assess compatibility and possibly enhance the aesthetic attributes of a relationship. Relationships should come together with the intense purpose of creating a free and loving environment. When in a loving relationship, one should feel safe, empowered, admired, adored, and unconditionally loved while subsequently being able to be free and accepted. Basking in the acceptance of the love of your life is an amazing feeling and is one that should be had by all.

How do you search for love when the love gene is dormant and unexplored, the lust and chemistry attraction gene is exploited all over the place, but that love thing does not get any play in the education department? It is my belief that learned behavior from our surroundings and family dynamics have a profound impact on our perception of relationships. When a relationship loses its shine, the glitter is gone, and all that you liked about one another dim so dark it hurts to stay in each other's company.

It appears this is the perfect time to talk to any and every noncounselor person that comes along your path, from friends to strangers. While on the train trying to get to their destination in peace, the dreaded questions come about how awful the other person is. The expectation becomes, "Look and listen to me, and see how valid my concerns are." Unbeknownst to you, the person being solicited for advice has never had a relationship beyond five months yet is being solicited to impart their wisdom on the unsuspecting question because you are desperately seeking advice on what went wrong and how the blame should not fall on their shoulders because they tried so hard. At some point in the conversation, you are given an in-depth description of how often the attempts to resurrect your relationship have fallen on death's ear.

The flip side of all this is the individual who is on the prowl for answers and is willing to be with any and everybody except the person they are committed to. This unwillingness to be with the primary partner may stem from a variety of excuses: boredom, loss of all interest in the lover because the intentions were not sincere, or a host of other items.

Many of us date our parents unconsciously, and we are replaying that parent-child tug-of-war with our partners. Our partners are generally unaware of their new role as surrogate parent and the part that they play in our relationship drama. With careful recognition and taking the fog off your eyes to really see what is going on, with the parental dynamic playing in the background, how can real intimacy develop and mature in a relationship? Most people have an innate desire to be in emotionally fulfilling relationships. The desire is such that no person is on an island all by themselves, being admired from a distance and never truly being touched or understood. While people crave intimacy, at the crux of it, they just want to feel safe on the mental, physical, and emotional plane. Ironically, that feeling can be very similar to that of parental care. You see this behavior all the time. However, it can be unrecognizable when adult children leave the nest and come back home indefinitely. The rejections of life may be overwhelming, and some may not have the strength to address and overcome their failed relationship. All it takes is that overnurturing parent to stunt the emotional growth of a child.

Movies and romance novels have made the idea of love appear easy since the self-help books have entered the market and have been on the roll with assisting the massive amounts of couples on how to conduct themselves in relationships.

Let's not forget the role magazines play in all the love talk, where it is easy to have access to anyone. It does not matter if you are shopping, pumping gas, on the way to work, at the bus stands, at the newsstands, drinking a cup coffee, eating a bagel, on your tablets, cell phones, and even waiting in a physician's office—you are accessible. People often use an invisible label with the headline of how to get and sustain love, and right beside the headlines is another headline, who breaks up with who and multimillion-dollar settlement in who keeps what. Really (as my daughter would say).

Relationships are intimate, but what is intimacy? Intimacy is a close feeling of being loved, needed, valued, understood, and affirmed. The awareness of your needs as a human being truly allows you to let another person in, which is supposed to be rich and fulfilling. All the while you are strengthening the delectable parts of your inner being that others do not have the privilege to see. That is the beauty of real intimacy: no longer feeling vulnerable, and ego feelings are thrown out of the window.

Wee! At last, I can be myself, but what if you do not know who you are based on this invisible parental tug-of-war under the radar of emotions? My theory is, after 90 to 160 days, the real you shows and the representative falls away. All bets are off, and the representative is now out of the building. The person you met disappears, and in walks the person you asked for.

Who is the representative? The representative is the first face you see, and that face is impressive. You cannot see divorces, children, extramarital relationships, outside children, drug habit, all habits, infidelity of every kind, embezzler, and thief at first. No, you cannot see the core self initially because the representative usually has all those sugary words of flattery and compliments and silk flowing off his or her tongue. Yes, sweetheart, over-the-top bravado dripping with confidence, the representative is either male or female. This link of false self covers up all the negativity that has been bestowed on them by exes or family members who have berated this such individual so that person is hidden away.

The nice representative comes forth because everyone needs an introductory face to who they are, and that is why "the representative" comes forth. Many people are not fortunate to have a double introduction, which means an actual person introducing you to the new person in question. The introduction usually comes with a monologue of all their good points, which are flawless. The second representative is the individual themselves giving blow-by-blow plays on their likes and dislikes—sometimes what they did not like about their last relationship, which gets subliminally planted into your psyche. Usually it gives the opposite effect, which is more of the same in your personal relationship with him or her.

This is the reason why it is so much easier to have hot sex with someone you would not see again because less work is involved that does not complicate with your niceties. When you get right down to it, men and women see things differently. We all know now why Mars-versus-Venus propaganda has been so popular, but what I have seen in my twenty-year practice is, men want intimacy in some cases more than it is led to believe. There are women in some other cases who only want to have a good time and be flattered, spoiled, and given some really powerful orgasms. When it gets tough, there are some women who are ready to flee; it is not just men.

In a relationship, the real parts of intimacy are feelings, touching, seeing, smelling, and communicating. The euphoria at the beginning of relationships, people do a replica to explore intimacy. Although it is ironic, a relationship starts with the cute, crazy, and cuddly phase.

INSIGHT WITHOUT CHANGE IS MEANINGLESS

At this point, the words that come out of their mouth is lovely and full of laugher. It is infectious, and it spews all over the place. Right, I call this the kiss, kiss, feel, feel, cannot get enough of you, "I love you, babe" phase. Well, 120 days or six months comes to an end, and some tarnish begins to appear; you would begin to notice small things happening, such as conversations taking place that you are not aware of, how the interaction with family is going, how work ethics affect the individual, and the interaction with their children. Nevertheless, in regard to the money, you start to wonder how they pay their bills or their generosity toward you.

Now we see more into the mechanisms of the relationship. Not quite so cute, but you can work with it, right? *Right?* Better! The reason why you can work with the relationship is that you gave in to the excitement and the arousal of anticipation of what this relationship could possibly bring in life. Once you verbally announce your "I don't like" regarding sex, it will complicate getting to know that person (unless getting to know them is really not the goal). This is when confusion comes into play and alters your emotional state of mind, especially if you have been in a drought (without a sexual companion) for a long time.

The first 120 days upon encountering a person of interest, those moments are laced with oxytocin hormone, which quickly reels you in for more and more exciting moments. So that first kiss is sexy and sensual, or sometimes not-so-sexy dopamine still sets in. Then you have become the best teacher in the sexy kissing contest.

When you have dopamine (adrenalin hormone) and oxytocin (the feel-good hormone) going on, your nerve cells are affected, and their hormones are going crazy. People have made many mistakes in relationships because the brain is off course, and in some cases, women start to shut down. It all depends on how good the orgasms is, which is entirely another story.

A Love Quiz

By answering the following questions allows you to determine if you are really ready to invest your whole self into a commitment of love despite all the tragedies you may have read in the tabloids while standing in line at the grocery stores. The tabloids attacks one wealthy tragedy after another. Especially when the wealthy cannot keep a good relationship, the questions resurface: How do people expect an average working-class individual to survive love? Let us be shown the path for love, and real love will surrender all known and unknown behavior for the pursuit of love.

Here we go. These are some questions that can be answered by you and the person you care about. The answers to these questions will help you with an honest assessment of your view of love. These questions will give you insight on what needs to change, or what you stand by in loving yourself or another individual.

- Is anyone a little happier because I came along today?
- Did I leave any concrete evidence of my kindness, any sign of my love?
- Did I try to think of someone I know in a more positive light?
- Did I help someone to feel joy, to laugh, or at least to smile?
- Have I attempted to remove a little of the rust that is corroding my relationships?
- Have I forgiven others for being less than perfect?
- Have I forgiven myself (hmm)?

INSIGHT WITHOUT CHANGE IS MEANINGLESS

- Have I forgiven my parent(s) (hmm)?
- Have I forgiven any persons that hurt me?
- Do I know the difference between obsession and love?
- Have I loved myself?
- Have I loved all my family?
- What does unconditional love mean?
- Have I learned something new about life, living, or love?
- Have I gone through the day without fretting over what I don't have and celebrating the things I do have?

If you are not satisfied with your answers, relax, breathe in and out. Tomorrow you may want to start the quiz over again! This is one quiz you can never fail.

My daily interactions are with people seeking answers to resolve a situation or problem they may encounter. On the following pages are questions that were presented to me for answers. I have answered these questions in a detailed fashion with the most optimum form of solutions for the person to find ways to take control of their own lives, as well as making an assessment on the situation that allows the person to experience a higher level of happiness with ease.

Foreword

What seems to matter to many of us is to not be alone. If you allow this all-consuming feeling to absorb all of who you are, then nothing in front of you may seem real, or your accomplishments do not light you up because what you are really striving for is a relationship. To experience that feeling takes away the whispers inside you that makes you feel whole and complete, so if that is what the anxiety is all about, you are wasting precious time. By not being willing to invest in you, you are not discovering you're actually beautiful. You are relinquishing all those doubts, fears, and disbeliefs that are clouding your real intentions. You need to trailblaze ahead in full force with confidence to be your best self.

In my practice, I see all types of individuals; many, many come back to give me updates and testimonials all regarding our session together. One, in particular, was intriguing: I had a client that said everything I said in our talks had happened verbatim. In our conversation, I told this woman she would meet an oh-so-wonderful guy, and he would completely sweep her off her feet. Everything she ever thought about, such as going on romantic trips and surprises of all kinds of jewelry, friends, and boat loads of money flowing into her life, came true.

After her messy divorce five years ago, she met him. He was the CEO of a company, and she was a scientist of infectious diseases. If Cinderella existed, she was definitely her. She was proposed to with doves and men singing while onlookers jumped for joy in amazement—an outdoor proposal brandishing festive lights of Christmas on display, a horse and carriage waiting with champagne for when she said yes. My client was everything her new fiancée desired because she was so easy to be with and never complained during the whole courtship. He fell in love with her because she allowed the magic to happen without interjecting an opinion. So he poured it on thick because he was a hopeless romantic and extremist. He never wanted the bubbles to end. Nightly gatherings and weekend functions were continued while trying to plan a wedding.

The wedding ended up costing $250,000, and yes, her fiancée didn't mind or break a sweat to pay for the entire wedding with all the bells and whistles for his bride. At her wedding, none of the bridesmaids had to purchase their dresses or shoes, and they got to keep their dresses after the wedding. Throughout the day and night the wedding was magical. They had the best-tasting food and lavish cocktails you could have imagined. You can view this wonderful wedding on YouTube. She was extremely beautiful. This client of mine was coming to me for help. She did not want to be alone for the rest of her life, neither did she want to raise her kids being alone. I told her, "No, never the case of you being alone for the rest of your life. You have so much to offer, and you are beautiful."

When you shift your thinking and start the practice of forgiving and releasing, happiness unfolds—to forgive and not forget as so many people do—it ultimately always leads to unhappiness. So my client started the process to forgive and release by writing a gratitude letter. She wrote on a sheet of paper names, circumstances, occurrences, and the understanding of why this individual was a part of her life lessons. She got the lessons in full effect and no longer needed to repeat the lesson over again. She ended it with the rituals of forgiving herself for taking so long to get the lesson. Then she forgave herself, proceeding to give thanks to the individual that put her though some difficult changes (what she calls "hell and back").

After writing the letter that had almost twenty-five people on the list, now she is capable of moving forward. This is one of a few tactics to help individuals to move on to the next level of their lives. Well, it's not always a one-stop shop; sometimes you need a maintenance visit to get you back on track.

I have foreseen more weddings during my practice than the individuals I helped have seen for themselves of the hope of ever getting married. I have had at least 180-plus clients get married over the years and got invited to five of them. I went to give my support to the couples, but only five; I am not mad. I'm just saying.

What is Love?

My answer is, the complete absence of fear. If you are in a relationship looking for escape clauses to use "just in case," then you have moved into doubt zone, acting on a disbelief in real happiness, and now fear is firmly in place. These emotions will surely bring in absolute reason to have an escape clause, which will be used. The questions that have been presented to me in whole or part were answered completely.

What I saw that were left out of some of the questions were given an extensive pulling out. I usually can see the whole scenario of the question, which undoubtedly are usually left out of the given questions. Questions are asked, which is fine, but the issue of the question is not what the questioner wants to know. The questioner wants a happy, positive solution to the sometimes-unthinkable problems. The real issue has not been given, so to better understand my answers given to the questioner, I may have to interject what I see, which adds more to the answer than the individual anticipated. To not confuse you, you may not actually understand why I have asked the question that I am bringing into the fold. Normally, I go in deeper to address the question because some issues, in order for the questioner to get all they should out of the answer, I need to excavate the scene around the issue and pull out some truths and untruths that were conveniently left out. I hope you understand that.

Allow me to answer your issue.

Issue 1: Love Caribbean-Style

My name is Shanell. I am so happy with my life. I got a promotion, and I am now traveling more with my girlfriends. We are having lots of fun on our girl trips. I used to be the type of person that is all work and no play. Finally, I am taking some time for me. My three-year relationship was in need of an overhaul. His name is Jack, and I told him that I am not going any further in the relationship once the new year comes in. I put up with his three teenage kids and two baby mommas for three years, and I am fed up. I told Jack that we needed to take our relationship to the next level, which, for me, is marriage, of course. I told Jack about my thoughts on marriage at the beginning of the year.

INSIGHT WITHOUT CHANGE IS MEANINGLESS

However, I have some concerns. It is now August, and I am having the time of my life. I met a young man in Nassau, Bahamas. Although I know this relationship with the young man is not going anywhere, my relationship with Jack had me thinking. Lately I have been feeling sexy and free. I want to be in a drama-free environment with effortless communication while being in a relationship and not being taken for granted. I want to have a regular sex life. Hell, I am forty-two years old, and I am not dead. To sum up this story, my boyfriend, Jack, bought a ring and is going to propose to me. I am pretty sure he will ask me to marry him soon, but I want to break up with my boyfriend. I desire to be with someone who is more attentive and does not have the baby-momma drama.

Ms. Dorothea, what should I do?

Answer 1: Shanell, I like that you have a mind of your own. Sometimes an insignificant event can change your perspective on how you would like to spend the rest of your life. It looks like Nassau was good to you and has given you an epiphany or two. I hope you know that he is a fling, a boy toy, and an illusion. If you and he were to get together seriously, he would be all in your bank account, trying to stay in luxury dress wear on your dime so he could pull in some twentysomething pretty young thing. You are feeling sexy because he makes you feel sexy. I ask you, Did you feel sexy before meeting him, and can you continue to feel sexy after he is long gone?

The real goal at hand is keeping you in a feel-good mode about yourself and coming to a conclusion about what makes you happy, especially if you're going to spend the rest of your life with him. Your three-year relationship does need some help in the commitment department, but his almost-grown teenagers are about to leave the nest. While child support will be less, it depends on the arrangements made with the mothers of the children. You have a choice now to contour this relationship as you want it. It is obvious he is not going anywhere, and in your early courtship, his infidelity was rampant. He is lucky you are still around. You have helped him grow and learn to appreciate a good woman. The ups and downs of a relationship do not mean the end; it can very well be the beginning. Give some consideration before giving him up and taking on the fancy fake feelings of a young buck.

Shift tools 1: Keep the sexy going. Mirror work—look in a full-length mirror butt naked (completely nude), look at yourself with a smile, not one frown, and say, "I love my head. I love my eyes. I love my nose. I love my cheeks. I love my lips. (You can embellish as you go on, for example: I love the way my eyes look. My eyes gives me a come-hither look, or I have sultry, bedroom eyes.) I love my chin. I love my neck. I love my shoulders. I love just the way my breasts look. I love my arms, even my upper arms are sexy too." (Smile and blow a kiss to the mirror.) Love your stomach all the way down to your toes and in between. Do often, and this increasingly grows that sexy self-esteem, and you would not have to grab a convenient opportunist to keep you company. You will attract a well-deserved, compatible love interest.

Affirmations 1: I love myself. I am well loved and cherished by all. I am always receiving wonderful attention from loving, cherished-filled individuals that always have my best interest at heart.

Issue 2: Why Can't I Get What I Want?

What Is Wrong with Me?

I met this great guy while I was out with a friend. He is a chef, and he has piercing big blue eyes and dark hair, about six feet two inches, and gorgeous. We have been seeing each other for a couple of months now, and he becomes so belligerent when I question him about his day. He does not hold the door for me or help me get in or out of the car, which is something I have become accustomed to from being in a relationship. Last but not least, he is always late, and he makes plans with friends that we have in common, and I am not included. What should I do?

Answer 2: Well, I see you're impressed with his appearance, and he sounds like a delicious piece of eye candy that has gone stale. Everything good to look at is not good for you. He seems spoiled and is used to getting attention. He knows there will always be some woman going "gaga" over him, as if he is some pseudo-celebrity or a nice piece of veal. You are not included because he does not take sand to the beach. He never knows what potential woman he is going to meet. You also gave up the sex way too early for him. He did nothing to deserve or earn it.

Regarding his behavior, if he satisfies you, then maybe it's worth it, but I got a feeling he is a lazy lover. I see you have been on this dating track for a while, one guy stranger than the other. You realize you are attracting this behavior. There is little or no healing in between the kick-to-curb guy and the new guy on the playing field. You are uncomfortable being alone, and when you see girlfriends who are married and appear happy, the feeling of loneliness is overwhelming. Your more-perfect-fit guy is out there if you stop moving from a level of anxious to panic attack to get a man and stop competing with the lives of your girlfriends. Bottom line—get rid of him!

Shift tools 2: How to not feel desperate in your soul. I want you to stretch out your body for fifteen to twenty minutes in the morning after waking up and before going to bed. This is to get out any unknown tension that you may be harboring without realizing it. Breathe in deep, lick your lips, and blow out slowly (this cool sensation over your lips as you blow out releases a feeling of calm). Do this fifty times. Try to sit for twenty minutes with a guided-meditation audio keeping you in a serene, loving, and joyous state.

Affirmation 2: Love is full of beauty, rich sounds, wonderful laughter, compassion, joy, and harmony. Love is real. Love surrounds this world with all that I can see, taste, touch, and feel. I know it is available for all who want it, and I want it. I take part in the magic of love. I embrace loving myself and embrace the love in others. As I do this, love and I do a dance together, bringing in rich rewards for my life. One of the rewards is a loving male counterpart that fulfills me as I fulfill myself with adoration and compassion.

Issue 3: The One Time I Let My Guard Down

Hi, Dorothea. I know you know how tough it is for me to like anyone, let alone have him come to my home. Well, I met this handsome financial analyst who is gainfully employed, cooks, dresses well, drives a nice vehicle, has his own place, gave me more than one telephone number, has a great sense of humor, and can dance like nobody's business. Sounds great, huh? I have not been to his home yet, and we have been going out for nine months. I have not even stopped in front of it. If he leaves something home, he will go get it and then come back by and pick me up.

We have been late for a couple of functions because of this behavior. I told him it will save time taking me along; I will sit in the vehicle, and we can leave from there. All he did was smile, kiss me on my forehead and lips, and kept it moving. He either came back or asked me to drive to meet him at the venue. I like everything about him except this behavior. Now, I am not a twentysomething-year-old woman. I am educated and well diverse in languages, commentating, and fencing. My heart is fully invested in this man, and common sense is telling me that something is wrong. Does he have a man somewhere in the closet (which is the worst-case scenario), or does he live with a woman—worst, a wife? In all my research, I could not find evidence of a wife, but I do know where he lives; although I have not been to his house yet. Should I go to his home uninvited? Help, Joeleen.

Answer 3: Joeleen, Joeleen, Joeleen (smile). So he gave you more than one telephone number; I bet it was to his cell and work, or his work cell, but not to his home phone because he does have a landline. You ask him who was living in his home. Well, you cannot tell me. So let me tell you. *His wife*, yes, he has a wife, and she is expecting their third child, which you will see if you go uninvited.

The reason you could not find evidence of the marriage is that they were married out of the country, and yes, it should be filed at City Hall or in tax records. He has everything incorporated, and all is in his company's name. You are dessert, and she is the entrée; you are the thing that motivates him to endure the entrée. Basically, you are keeping him married for a long time. Otherwise, he would be thinking about getting out as soon as the third baby was spoken of.

He is so excited to see you, and because of that, he is happier around the house, more attentive to the kids and his wife. She really thinks he is on board with the news of the baby. I hope he is not in your bed when she delivers their third child. She is known to have late-night baby deliveries. I know you are afraid to ask and if you ask, he will tell you the truth, unfortunately. That is not the real problem; the real problem is what you are going to do. Your heart is fully invested, as you said. I do see you tempting to try to manage something despite you being the other woman and knowingly becoming the mistress.

Shift tools 3: Undue tight guard. Do some volunteer work, or connect with the pulse of the people in your community. There is a charity organization named "The Hearts and Souls of Humanity" that needs volunteers. Sit in on a divorce-recovery meeting and listen to the stories of women that have experienced their homes been broken apart because of women knowingly and unknowingly sleeping with married men. Help, inspire, listen, feed, and reorganize the hurt of disappointment from these women.

Acknowledge the souls of these women that may be temporarily lost or misguided. Then allow your presence to be the saving grace for one of them. This is an exercise of trust and release, allowing your heart chakra to open and take in all of what life has to offer. When your heart chakra opens, it will begin to shift your perspective of mankind, which got you in a state of loneliness and blindsided your guard.

Affirmations 3: The blooms on a flower blossom every season that allows the bees to do what is natural. Nature automatically knows what to do without resistance, just as love knows what to do. It is humans that get in the way of love. Love starts with self; self-love attracts healthy, loving partners. Self-love gives permission to love and will never steer me wrong. I am lovable. Everyone loves who I am, the way I am, and how I am. I love, love, love, loves me.

Issue 4: I Heard It, but I Did Not Believe It

Hi Dorothea. This is Tiffany A. You told me two years ago, but I did not believe it. We were so in love, but the no account son of a——is taking me to court for full custody of our son, which he does not want to pay child support for. Yes, you were right; he did get married, just like you said. It took me by surprise because we got mad at each other as we usually do and did not speak for a while. I would usually say whatever and hang up the phone. In a couple weeks or maybe less we would start talking again.

This time we stopped talking for almost a year. Although he still would come over to bring my son what he needs (except money), then he will leave. Now he is dropping this bullsh——t on me that he wants full custody of his son because he says I am unfit. He said he will prove that I am an unfit parent to the courts. I wish I could find the tape where you told me that the Negro will take me to court with his no-account, short-ass attention span.

Help, Ms. Dorothea. Give me some advice before I lose my composure and go and beat his motherf—cking ass. What am I to do? He is drowning me in all these attorney fees. He files motions every other week. I know somebody is in his ear, which could be that so-called wife. Help.

Answer 4: Tiffany, breathe in and out deeply twenty times right now. Feel the oxygen going in and out of your lungs. Stay present of your breath, not what could possibly happen in a day, a week, or even a month. Stay with me right now. Tiffany, get it together. This man knows how to push your buttons, and it is very easy to do so, given the nature of your history together, so please calm down.

When it comes time to go to court, he will purposely push your buttons in the courtroom for the judge to see the raving lunatic you can be in his presence. Although you and I know he is much worse. The court will only see a calm, patient, loving man with only the best interest of his son in mind. With his wife by his side, the two of them will look like pillars of the community, while you look like a dressed-up welfare recipient despite your education. Everything relies on you, so focus on an attorney that works on contingency. Your attorney will reverse your court fees on the case since he is filing so many useless documents, which says a lot about him.

Now, I do not see him getting full custody of your son. What I see is that you must keep your composure, so you get your son and explain to the courts why he should not get full custody. From what I can see, his strategy is to not pay child support. He thinks the courts giving him full custody will eliminate him from paying child support. He also hopes that the courts will award him joint custody, which will work in his favor. If he goes to court for full custody and gets joint custody, this still will work in his favor because he thinks equal custody means equal support. He does not want to pay you any money unless he voluntarily gives it to you.

Insurance for your son will need to be paid. I see that he may be ordered to pay for the insurance, along with any specialty organizations or sports your son belongs to. With that said, the arrangement may not be bad at all because your dating life comes back to life, and your son will be in a reliable home. Unfortunately, your ex will be upset, since life really begins for you and your son. Summers and weekends will be with his father and wife. They will have to pay for a sitter when they want to go out. In the end, it is comfortable when you release the present appearance of things.

Shift tools 4: Join a support group for single mothers who have both joint custody and sole custody. Interacting with the group can relieve your mind tremendously. Also, playdate groups for your son on meetup.com for single parents works really well.

Affirmation 4: I am a willing participant in my life to see it flow easily as I let the appearance of discord float down the river of life. I know life supports me in all that I do, and I accept what life has to offer.

INSIGHT WITHOUT CHANGE IS MEANINGLESS

Issue 5: A Seven-Year-Ago Talk Transpired

Hi, Ms. Dorothea. I spoke to you seven years ago, and it happened like you said: my ex is dead, and he left me a letter of apology. Even though we have been apart for twenty years, how do I get past this?

Answer 5: I feel your pain and grief, and this is not easy. You have been wondering off and on for the past twenty years what his true feelings were regarding you. You left this man because he was being stubborn and uncompromising. His behavior made you felt vindicated to leave this man when he did not honor your love for him the way you wanted him to. Youth is something else; he was young and silly at the time. Let's be honest, you never stopped loving this man. You threw your love and this relationship away.

Now twenty years have gone by, and you have not been in love since. Basically, you are feeling guilty that this man died without you swallowing your pride to tell him you never stopped loving him. Release the guilt and tell him you love him. He has crossed over, but the energy of him can hear and sense you. You know he loved you. Healing begins to take place.

Shift tools 5: Write a "dear God" letter, telling God about love lost, and then forgive yourself. Ask God what you could do get over the pain of lost love for human frailty. Send love to the remnants of love the two of you shared and send love to yourself.

Affirmation 5: I forgive myself for any shortcomings I may have. Life is a big classroom, and mistakes are a part of my life lessons. I can always correct a mistake with the release of guilt. I send love to my heart and to any soul or anyone I may have made a mistake to. I send love.

Issue 6: The Forbidden Has Gotten Me

Dorothea, I have a unique problem. I have fallen in love with my son's close friend. They are both in their last year of college and over twenty-one. I know I should be ashamed, but I cannot help these feelings. He and my son came home for a weekend. They have been home for many of the holidays and weekends. My husband thought they were gay, but I knew better.

My son's friend came into the kitchen where I was sitting at the table two in the morning. I was restless and couldn't sleep (I had a lot on my mind). I was drinking hot cocoa and with Godiva (your recipe), and I asked him if he would like a cup of cocoa. Yes, he replied. As I got up from the kitchen table, he walked closer to me and started kissing me oh-so passionately while his robe came undone. I almost fell to the floor. His penis was so big it did not look natural. His penis was sticking up out his robe between the two of us. I cannot let this go on. I made up my mind. I am not going to sleep with him, but I want to so badly. I won't, I can't, for my baby's sake, I won't.

Answer 6: You sound indecisive. I'm sure your son's friend is someone's baby as well. Isn't it true that when you and your son are together, there are times people mistake him for your boyfriend? You have a youthful flare about you, and you got married very early and had children rather young.

There was a time when girls were going to school, getting their degrees and getting dressed in the finest dresses, high heels, and stockings with a black seam up the back of the leg while drenching themselves in perfume and going to clubs. You watched and listened to the laughter as they closed their doors and got into their vehicles and drove off. Meanwhile, you were at home, rocking babies, keeping a house in order, and preparing your husband's dinner at the time, so much of your youth was given up to being a wife and mother.

Though you do not have any regrets about that, you still feel as though you missed out on the carefree lifestyle of a twentysomething woman. Not to dig up your past, but your parents, aunts, uncles, neighbors, friends, and pastor all tried to convince you to not get married just yet. They wanted you to wait a couple of years, but you were adamant that you wanted to get married, and you did. You raised three gorgeous children and still have a husband who loves and appreciates you.

With that being said, you look good for being married over twenty-three years. Most of the kids are almost grown, and you are rediscovering yourself as a sexual being, not just a mother and a wife. This is fine; however, I know you can find a healthier way of doing this without destroying a child in the process. I see you are going back to school and taking up those art classes you always wanted to do. Enrolling in an art-history class you love so much will get you back to expressing yourself. This will be good for you, anything but having sex with an inexperienced young man (or boy, since he is your son's age).

Do you see that you are repeating history all over again because of your libido, which is getting in the way again just as it did some twenty-three odd years ago? This time there are horrible consequences if continued in this direction. Your husband, for instance; consider the consequences of what would happen because the ego of your youthfulness is so out of control he will take everything from you with this adulterous affair.

Remember your young lover is living off his parents and cannot afford a place for the two of you to stay comfortably. Your life has been well provided for in this marriage. You will be penniless and have to go to your family while no one will understand this rich-to-rags choice because your family members were proud and envious of you and the love your husband showed you all the time in front of your family. So my suggestion is to get some counseling to talk out these feelings and even come in to talk to me so we can see some of the far-reaching possibilities or consequences.

Shift tools 6: Seek a change or life coach for beginning a new phase of your life. Seek a third-party counselor to help you and your husband shift into new lives, which will help with the guilt and resistance that is inevitable to come. Write down some of your talents and see which one you can capitalize on that can turn into a venture that is of service to others.

Affirmation 6: I am youthful and loving life right now. I make decisions based on who I am today. I choose love and freedom, the freedom to love my family and to love myself. Life morphs itself and my family into new experiences, and I am fine with new loving experiences. I choose life, love, and longevity. I give the gift of choice with the truth. I am free to be happy, loving, and adventurous.

Issue 7: Enough Is Enough, We Need to Get Married

I'm not doing this any longer. I am so tired of his tired excuses. I have been dating this man for a little over nine years, and it has been a struggle. He has always lived with his cousin, or he will move in with some other friends. We have season passes to the football games and always tailgate with a circle of friends we both know (his friends mainly) and socialize with everyone around us. He is the type of guy that wants to try and have his cake and eat it too. He hangs out all various times of the night, working jobs with his friends, where he is not bringing in the kind of money a man should make on a job. He is just living the frat-boy life without ever entering into somebody's college, and he is damn near forty-six years old. It's too much. I just found out people in his circle don't know I am his woman.

I'm tired of this treatment. I wish I could get him out my system and move on. I am always there for him whenever he needs me, and he is rarely there for me. I know how this sounds, but my heart would not let go. I feel like I am in prison because now I have his code to his phone, and he cannot lie to me anymore. I know what is going on, and still, I want us to grow and become an exclusive couple. Why is it that he cannot see we are good together and we should not throw these nine years away? We should move to the next level. What is wrong with him?

Answer 7: Wow, that is a lot, a whole lot. I do know this: you do not want to move on because in the beginning, you said nine years. The reason you do not want to move on is the fact you feel as though you are throwing nine years away, and you want something to show for your time invested in this relationship. You are getting older, and you feel you do not have that kind of time to just throw away (am I right or what?).

So you put up with a lot from this man, and what incentive does he have to change and treat you better? He would treat a new love better than you because her standards would be different than yours have been in this relationship. Therefore, his expectations would be different than what you were receiving. His new love would be about being a couple and being a couple only.

Your agenda was real marriage at any cost, so you gave your boyfriend rope without consequences or bottom line. You have in your favor your history together and he loves you, but now you have to compete with younger women, and everything he knows about you is passé. There is no incentive for marrying you. An ultimatum may not work, since that is what you have been thinking about. Try it, but do not be disappointed if you do not get the outcome you have been looking for.

Open communication with him on what it is you want and ask what it is he wants, then see if the two of you could meet in the middle based on the answers. Or you can find a vacation spot that focuses on rekindling relationships that have gone stale. More than likely he will not want to go on any type of vacation because he would rather work and hang out with his boys to drink. Book a singles cruise and begin the process of feeling desirable again. You will start to feel more desirable, especially with all the mature young well-built physique hunks beating your cabin door down for attention.

Shift tools 7: Healing retreats are great for you to undo the negative messages you are playing over and over in your head. Self-esteem building is needed for you not only in your relationship but in your job arena as well. With this retreat, networking will go on, and you will inevitably get a $60,000 raise in a new job as well. Spin classes to get rid of flab and imaginary flab.

Affirmation 7: I am never forsaken by love. The world is filled with love, and it lays at my feet like a bed of roses of opportunity to partake in my loving, floral life experience.

Issue 8: My Boyfriend of Four Years Wants A Baby, and I Think I Want to Give Him One. Am I Crazy?

My boyfriend of four years wants a baby, and I think I want to give him one. Am I crazy?

Answer 8: Straight crazy. Your boyfriend, correct me if I am wrong, he is a married man who will not get a divorce at all if he has a say in it. He is using you as a diversion to break up the monotony of his marriage. Now he has a teenage daughter already in the picture. What is she to think about this entire situation? Wait a minute, a *wife* who is still very much in the picture as well. *Hello.* This man will not respect you if you get pregnant, and there will be endless arguments about getting rid of the pregnancy. Ultimately, say goodbye to your boyfriend and say hello to the court system while trying to get child support from him. Why is he your boyfriend after four years? May I ask why you purposely stayed second in this man's life and yours? What, are you not deserving of bringing a child into this life while telling the baby it is not deserving as well? Painful.

Shift tools 8: Release your insecurities so you can attract and date mentally and emotionally available men. Look at the more than 100,000 dating sites waiting for you. There are single, handsome men that are available. You should consider speed dating, single cruises, single-travel groups, etc. Stop looking in the unavailable-man section of the internet. Stop being a disposable napkin and choose to be the whole tablecloth, which is around year after year.

Affirmation 8: I attract loving, mentally, emotionally, and physically available men who want me to be the *Mrs.* in their life, not their booty call, or get some in the back of their Jeep Cherokee. I deserve exclusivity because I love me.

Issue 9: Stay

All I ever hear is, "Stay the night. Why don't you stay the night? C'mon. I will fix breakfast for you in the morning. Why you have to leave so early? Let's talk and hold each other." I do not want to stay the night. I know I am separated from my wife, and we call ourselves working it out, but there is a woman I see during my separation named Trina.

Her house is so nasty I cannot even begin to sleep in her bed without thinking about what might crawl on me. The sex is like something that does not even exist in this world. She will allow me to experiment, and I am comfortable with her experimenting on me because it takes me to a level that I never had with my wife or any of my girlfriends from the past. Trina does not know the meaning of cleaning up anything, but she got some good loving. Damn, but I cannot stay but so many hours at her place.

I do prefer when we get a room, and she comes to my place for an evening (I got an apartment during my separation from the wife). I just do not like her at my place all the time because she gets too comfortable and starts hinting about leaving some clothes and shoes here and maybe a toothbrush and hair supplies. I just want to hit it as often as I can before my wife and I get back together, if we get back together.

This woman here cannot be the main lady. The sex is good, almost too good to give up, but hell, what is going to happen when I cannot perform in the bedroom or when she gets too old to perform? I do not want to be stuck with this package for the rest of my life. I know this sounds shallow, I know, but I am being truthful. I do care for my wife, but she has a big mouth, and I am tired of her as well; but we were together twenty-six years, and the kids are having a hard time with the separation, but hell, they are not kids anymore, and they need to get a life of their own. Hopefully, they will find a man that would marry them. One thing about my wife—she keeps a damn clean home; it is spotless. I can't keep this one. She gets offended when I tell her to clean up.

Answer 9: Ouch! Who said the truth doesn't hurt sometimes? You have to respect that. Get a life before you die of pancreatic cancer (metaphysical meaning) alone, and all you will have is getting close to your memories and funeral arrangements. You are being shallow; I hope you know this. Stop and take some classes in love or some counseling sessions alone to get to the heart of why you've been so unhappy (it is usually an unfulfilled accomplishment after being married so long).

The extras you can get between some woman's legs do not always make you happy long-term. Maybe you should get back out there. If you do not believe me, have a conversation with some men that have left their family for an extra piece on the side. See if they tell you about their experience of long-term happiness with the sidepiece. Then look at all the old sick men who died alone without the benefit of choosing love or threw love away because of the one-hundred-plus shallow reasons.

Shift tools 9: Love classes. Enroll into a men's support group or join the many Spiritual Living Centers of Atlanta to do some volunteer work with homeless men shelters and with injured vets.

Affirmation 9: I am love. Therefore, I attract love. I cannot draw in what I am not. I am the wonderful, loving, charismatic package of love.

Issue 10: I Have Been with My Boyfriend for Eleven Years. Is He the One for Me?

Hi, Ms. Dorothea. My boyfriend has been with me for eleven years, and I want to see where this relationship is going.

Answer 10: Your relationship has been marked with many birthdays, which have been eaten alive like a Pac-Man game. Infidelity has been an issue on both your sides of the relationship. You have both been unfaithful and outraged when you suspected he is cheating. Each of you plays the tit-for-tat game of unfaithfulness. The question should not be, Is he the one for me? The question should be, am I deserving of a better man in my life, or do I want to be a better person for myself? Where did you get Elmer's Glue that keeps you stuck in pain? It is time for a serious reassessment about getting out of this relationship so you can start learning to love yourself, which falling in love with you will ultimately bring in a wonderful new love.

Shift tools 10: Read books about healthy, whole relationships. Take some free basic human-nature classes at a local college. Join meetup.com groups with meetings based on creating a better you, and join the ones that do guided meditation. Yoga will help an energy shift as well.

Affirmation 10: There is something inside me that knows what I deserve. It reaches out to me like the sun peering through a cloudy day. As a rainbow appears through those lifting clouds, life tells me it will be okay and life has my back. I can be free to choose love. What a beautiful, clear day of choice and love on my path.

Issue # 11: He's Separated, Not Divorced

Hi, Ms. Dorothea. I've been wondering if I should continue to pursue this married man. He lives alone. He says he is separated and not yet divorced. In fact, he has not mentioned when he will be divorced, or if they are in the process at all. I like him so far, but I am not trying to get my feelings entangled in him if this relationship is not going anywhere. What do you think I should do?

Answer 11: He said married, and I do not understand why there was more conversation after that. Married and separated means you have unfinished business. He needs to finish the process, but he chooses to be out trying to make love connections while still having a wife hanging around somewhere. This is dangerous, but would it be his fault or your fault if a brick went through your car window while you are sitting on his sofa with her (unfinished business) husband?

Let me give you a little insight: he is still talking and interacting with the original girlfriend, the woman he was cheating with, which got him kicked out of his home, who just told him she is pregnant. Your new man's wife that is separated from her husband does not know about the pregnant woman. She is super angry he cheated on her with her cousin while she is carrying his baby. He now has two women pregnant and upset with himself. The drama has not happened yet. This man is about to ask you for a loan to help pay for an abortion for the girlfriend, which she will not get, and your money will not be returned. Run.

Shift tools 11: To stop attracting deadbeats. Make a list of qualities you would like to have in a man, and if you see "married" on the list, cross it out and add an emotionally, mentally, physically, and available relationship-minded gentleman. Describe a man who knows that his financial life has to be just as intact as his physical health. A man that is proud of his accomplishment and demonstrates professionalism while working on his job. Attract a man who loves his mother and would not drag women's self-esteem through the mud because he values being raised by a queen who taught him the meaning of respect of all women, even those who lack respect for themselves. Feel you are worthy of an emotionally available, unattached man. Then you know it.

Affirmation 11: I love and respect me. Therefore, anyone who pursues me will cherish me as I cherish myself. Love and understanding are at the forefront of the minds of the individuals who pursue me. I am sexy, sassy, loving, and well deserving of wonderful love, and so it is.

Issue #12: I Survived Cancer, Now I Want Out

For years I have been feeling claustrophobic in my marriage. My obligations were overwhelming. However, I succeeded in my duties as a wife, mother, employee, and daughter-in-law. My illness reminded me of who I use to be, which was a person with great aspirations. I wanted to see the world and act on Broadway to become an actress.

However, I became a wife and mother to a loving family that has given me the zest to live life. I do not want to feel guilty anymore. I want to have the ability to be fulfilled and happy. I have a good husband, but I have never been happy… grateful but not happy. Surviving cancer has been a wonderful awakening in my life. I have been able to see how miserable I was giving to everyone but myself. I feel the best way to thank the doctors is to do something with my life for me. I need some direction…an answer…help…I'm drowning.

Answer 12: You are a triumph to all survivors because you are not going back to your uncomfortable grooves. You are seeking more out of life because this is a second chance. The great thing about that is you recognize it as a second chance at life. Take life by the horns. Release guilt by seeing your situation for as debilitating as it was. You have grown people all around you, and if they do not know how to survive without you in a crisis, then they will need to learn.

This survival, or as I call independence, can and must continue. If you must remind the adults in your home that you want your life, give them directions to the information age of the Internet and have them google "how to get a life of your own." In order to enjoy the rest of your life stress-free, then so be it. This is what I know: you have to want the best for you in order for them to want the best for themselves. Be the example.

Shift tools 12: Art therapy classes, acting classes, or comedy classes to keep you laughing and motivated. Tell your story through laughter. Join Toastmasters and pursue motivational speaking. Be bold and tell your inspiring story of second chance.

Affirmation 12: I am alive, and I love it. I breathe easy, and I love it. I express who I am in healthy and creative ways, and I love it.

Issue 13: My Ex-Husband Is a Prick and a Wealthy One

My ex-husband has a wealthy father that does not really tolerate him. My ex has always been an alcoholic, drug-addicted asshole and the biggest womanizer in the world. My ex-father-in-law is a celebrated painter and has always given his grandchildren original artwork for Christmas. I have been divorced for five years, and for the last two years my children have not received any gifts from their grandfather. He is an intimidating, stick-in-the-mud, grumpy, mean-ass man.

However, he has a sweet, wonderful wife. She used to be my mother-in-law and advocate. She was the best part of my marriage, but she is a saint, and I could not duplicate that life she demonstrated with her asshole-ish husband. They produced a nontalented asshole-ish, drug-addicted son who happens to be my children's father. All I want is my children's fair share. I do not want them to be cut out of their inheritance, which the other grandchildren continue to get every year.

Answer 13: Believe it or not, once you got divorced, your in-laws pretty much stopped thinking about you. Unfortunately, your ex-husband's lack of activity in your children's life dictated the grandfather's activity and interest. The grandfather became oblivious to your children and is content to live his life with his immediate family. You, my dear, must remember your ex-father-in-law is not a warm man and prefers to be a little reclusive.

Now, the saving grace is that your semi-adult children or adult children can get all that is coming to them if they stay connected to their grandparents by visiting, calling, e-mailing, and sending cards and letters on birthdays and anniversaries. Their Christmas gifts will return immediately. Your coddling and influencing your children through estrangement due to your bitter divorce, coupled with being thrown back in the dating world, has rattled you, and I see you are not happy about that.

Shift tools 13: Visualize the love between you and your ex-in-laws. Visually see yourself sending love to your ex-husband and his parents. Stand still with soft music in the background. Place your hand on your heart and remember experiencing the miracle of birthing your babies into the world and your first glance of falling in love with them. Allow that love to swell in your heart and imagine that love being sent out in an invisible stream to the people you are uncomfortable with. Practice this daily until it becomes second nature to you. Once it becomes second nature, you will do it automatically anytime a difficult situation or tragedy occurs.

Affirmation 13: I release all anxiety and thoughts of my children being taken advantage of. I send love to my in-laws, and I stay in touch without an agenda or malice. Love sanitizes the old pain and discomforts. I choose love.

Issue 14: Thirty-Four Years and Counting

I cannot seem to keep a good man in my life. The men I have encountered have been users. Some of my friends have terrible men in their lives. I grew up around poverty, and there were many men who either were unemployed or had physical-labor jobs. Many of the women in their lives were the breadwinners, which bred contempt and left the women without the much-needed acknowledgment from their men.

Abuse was rampant, as many men were hungry for an opportunity, angry, and frustrated that they had very little money. The men took their frustrations out on their women or wives for those who actually got married. Although a horrible cycle, I still managed to get my degree and land a good job. Yet I still continue to get men who do not have a problem asking me for money or any type of assistance as if their ability to take care of themselves has disappeared. Is this my fate? There has yet to be a man in my life that has been a knight in shining armor as many women may dream. I have my master's degree and make close to six figures, but the only men I meet are blue-collar workers, unemployed, and losers. Why is that?

Answer 14: It is evident that seeds were planted before your birth and have continued to sprout throughout your adolescence until now. You may ask, *What are the seeds that were planted?* Let me explain to you what was reinforced all around you and throughout your plethora of experiences. Many men have perceived that women had the opportunity to go as far as they choose, but the cycle for black men is continuously denied, and that burden needs to be lifted.

Women had no choice but to step up to the plate, bring the bacon home, cook it, and serve it. Women had to take care of the needs of both their men and children, ultimately becoming the main stage of the family. The feeling of inferiority started eating away at the males while women depended on the system or handouts to get by. Many men felt the same way when a woman could get a job anytime doing domestic work, taking care of children, working in hospitals as nursing aids, and eventually going to school for nursing while living a life of chaos. Women did not want the worst-case scenario of being alone. Invisible, unspoken seeds were planted, and growing those seeds were called emotional abandonment or fear of abandonment.

So a dirty pair of pants lying next to you was better than having no pair of pants to launder and/or repair. Some black men became cold and unfeeling and found ways to take care of themselves by exploiting women because of hate. The men needed to feel superior over the women who appeared to take away their masculinity and dominate them. The goal became to get them young and weak and pounce on them with their dominant ways. This routine was continually present in families, surrounding neighborhoods, and in the families of your classmates and friends. Uproot those seeds, know a better life, know what you deserve, and know that you are going to get the desired life. This is not your fate.

Shift tools 14: Forgive the pain of the past and bless it for getting you through. Be thankful you were strong and intelligent enough to recognize it for what it was. Start healing you. See your worth and know you do not have to settle because you are worth loving on an equal level. Write down exactly what it is you want in a wholesome, loving relationship. Know what it takes to create this relationship.

If you do not know, investigate some models of relationships that have the dynamics you are looking for by asking questions or just do research. Make improvements to yourself so you can draw in what it is you exactly want; get your mind, body, and spirit together. There are several ways to get this done. You can start taking classes to get your body the way you want by healthy eating. Take classes on nutrition and start getting into the mindset of reinforcing to yourself that you are a magnet to your divine right match. Meditate or do yoga.

The magic of being quiet is key to the transformation of your life. Start joining groups on how to script your better life so you can learn to shift your thoughts and beliefs. Get back into your passion. You wanted to be an actress at one time; well, now is the time to take some acting classes. The reality may be crying and just balling your eyes out and releasing false beliefs you had about yourself that did not bring you your desired outcomes. Once this release has taken effect, you can get to the business of really living faithfully.

Affirmation 14: I release the bum magnet I created for myself. I affirm a healthy, whole, loving relationship with joy and intimacy of being genuine in getting to know me and feeling peace in the process.

Issue 15: Passionless Marriage

I met someone who is very powerful, sexy, and rich. He was some kind of fluke. I went to a beach house with my sister and a good friend of hers. I wanted to drown my trouble in Chardonnay and Chardonnay and more Chardonnay. I was doing a pretty good job of it until the vacant house down the way on a further stretch of beach became occupied with a dark-haired man with salt-and-pepper streaks.

While walking on the beach with my wineglass, I saw him cleaning and putting some trash out. We both waved at each other as I continued to walk in the sand. The beach tide was moving in and out over my feet, my pant legs were getting wet, and my glass was out of Chardonnay. I turned around and headed back to my sister's friend's beach house. The dark-haired man was outside his beach house with a wineglass and a bottle of wine, motioning me to come over.

He was speaking, but I could not hear him; curious, I went toward him. He had Gershwin wine in the bottle, a more seductive and delicious taste than I had. The wine was not too sweet or bitter; neutral-tasting, but crisp; a tad bit of sparkling was added, or it was the company. I found myself talking to the stranger. I felt an increased warmth and familiarity during our conversation. His smile was enchanting, and he lifted my glass with such grace. We toasted with each new fill until the bottle was empty. I was not sluggish or tipsy. He walked me back to my friend's beach house and kissed me on the cheek.

My sister has been wondering where I had been disappearing for the last couple of days. Well, the gentleman I met was named Charlie. Charlie and I had really been getting acquainted in a nonsexual way until the last day of my visit. I turned my cell phone off for some reason, and we drank wine. He had cases of this stuff. He wanted to write his novel and planned to stay until the novel was finished, but a crisis arose at his firm, and he was packing up. We laughed and talked. I loved his sense of humor, and his culinary skills were to die for. Cooking was his way to relax, and he relaxed well.

So I am beating around the bush; we eventually made love—so cliché—on the floor in front of the fireplace while listening to the waves crash in and out. So that is how he did it, in and out. It was wild and crazy and passionate, something I never experienced with my husband or any other man. I am back in the reality of my life. I have been home from the beach now two months, and I think that man slipped me some crack because I cannot stop pacing and thinking about him. My husband does not understand why dinner has not been prepared on time in weeks. I have called Charlie twice, and he has not returned my calls.

What should I do, or what is to become of me, since I am having Charlie withdrawals? Also, this does not have anything to do with me and is purely a speculation, but I think my sister is gay. She and her friend are really close, and I could swear I saw my sister's lipstick smudged on the corner of her friend's lips. Additionally, very late one evening I heard voices in the bathroom, and the water was running, and I opened the door a crack and did not see anyone. When I said, "Is anybody in there?" the bathroom went silent. I just threw that out there. My situation is hopeless; my husband and I have not made love in about two years, and now it does not faze me. I do not want to, and it has never been good. I am an opened bloom in the shadow of what I had experienced to this reality.

Answer 15: I see you are poetic. Charlie was overwhelmed by you; you were such a distraction to him. You were beautiful, funny, compassionate, a team player, and a playful gift from heaven—such a wild card. He never imagined a woman like you existed. (To me, some of that was a love-starvation high; the dopamine in you was off the charts.) He was hoping to start or finish a book in solitude, which was his goal. He is keeping to his deadline for himself now that you are gone. Your beach lover is full of complications.

His plan is to never see you again because he cannot give up his family no matter how unhappy he is. He is in it for life. Memories of you crowd his mind daily, and I promise one day you will hear from him, but I see it could be anywhere from two months to two years from now. Do not get excited; nothing will come of it. Your sister, on the other hand, has been sleeping with women for years. She and her friend have been a so-called couple for two years. I do not see the friend getting a divorce any time soon on her end. She will inadvertently call out your sister's name while making love to her husband. Now that is when it gets to be interesting. Have you just noticed their friendship?

Shift tools 15: To bring back the passion in your marriage, there are classes for Kama Sutra, tantric, couples' massage, romantic cooking, and wine tasting with eight-course meals for couples. If you begin to shift your energy and make an effort, your husband will follow your lead.

Affirmation 15: I have a whole lot of living to live. I am willing to participate in my marriage to find the good in it while moving toward a healthy future with the promise of love and affection to rekindle.

Issue 16: They Called Me Purposely Too Late

I am fortunate to have a job with a promising career. Many women in my shoes that are dating drug dealers do not usually work. Based on my observation, they appear to be dependent on their man for everything. I was not trying to date and either fall in love with a drug dealer; it just happened. This man has always tried to reassure me that he had my back. I know he is not going to be in this relationship for the long haul. However, he furnished my house and bought me some nice vehicles. My contribution has been helping him raise two of his kids along with mine. His kids and his family loved me, as well as his extended family.

An argument with my boyfriend's cousin and the cousin's friend turned into a deadly shooting. My boyfriend was the person that was shot. The bullet pierced a vein or artery, and he bled to death before arriving at the hospital. Once he arrived at the hospital and was pronounced dead is when everything turned around with his family and me.

The family locked me out of the house. I lived in with my boyfriend for five years. They took his keys, stole the cars, and

INSIGHT WITHOUT CHANGE IS MEANINGLESS

parked them somewhere else where I could not have access to them. His family has treated me like a stranger. The only thing I could do is retrieve my children, clothes (escorted by the police), and was not allowed to take anything else. I couldn't even get my jewelry, any decor from the house, pots, pans, and my mother's genuine silverware. I could not claim the cars since they were not in my name.

The cars were not in his name, neither it was in his business partner and best friend's name. My boyfriend just paid the loan. I have been getting threatening calls from my boyfriend's older kids, which it is hard to believe because we were so close. I cannot get into my home. My boyfriend has always kept money in the house, and his family or older sons know this, so that is why I can't go in. My life is in turmoil; the love of my life is dead. I am here alone, trying to figure it all out. Ms. Dorothea, let me know what is in my best interest.

Answer 16: The street life has laws of itself, as you well know. Your boyfriend was a hustler and, to some degree, ruined the lives of many families with what he was selling. You reaped the benefits of this type of labor-intensive career he had, and you stood idly by his side, doing nothing to give back to the community or talk him out of his career where he would have actually listened.

Karma comes home to roost, which means you get back what you put out, and it has to come back in this form. Your life has been ruined. You have been stripped of everything, even your purchases with your hard-honest money and his earned income. Everything that you obtained with and without the boyfriend—his family is treating the possession like he provided it all.

It is the same premise as the customers who stole from their families to purchase the service your boyfriend provided. The boyfriend's family has put things in perspective so that you can understand. You may say you did not sell anyone anything, but you did if you took the money to go shopping at the expense of all the victims. You may have to leave town because now death threats are coming for you because of association, and people believe you have a lot of money or know where it is located.

The sheer thought of his family thinking that you have something to do with the money they will no longer receive. As hard as it may be, it is time to move on with your life, and the erasure of five-plus years is hard enough, all while grieving the loss of your love. This is not worth leaving your two babies behind in exchange for a grave. You are a smart cookie and wear a gold reminder around your neck, which is pretty smart on your end to remind you of a safe-deposit box that only you and your boyfriend knew about.

What about the insurance policies you insisted on when the two of you started dating? He only agreed to it because he needed a lot of that money going somewhere, and those policies were automatically paid, and paperless mail went to your email, not his. Have you forgotten? They have been paid up to date—all three policies. The question is, Will you keep your promise by giving his family some money in the event something happened to him?

Shift tools 16: Remember, your prayers are always answered, and sometimes the answer does not come in the form the way you may want. Continual prayer work and forgiveness work for your boyfriend and all parties involved. Everyone who was a part of your boyfriend's circle, including the family, has been forever shifted, including you. A book recommended to read is "12 Steps of Forgiveness" by Paul Ferrini; it is a good place for you to start.

Affirmation 16: I attract a love of wholesome ideas that is wonderful to me, and I will continue to attract a love for my highest and best good under grace and in a perfect way.

Issue 17: Why Is He Still Calling Me?

Hi, my name is Diane. My husband left, or should I say abandoned his children and me. He is staying across town with this other woman, who is buying him whatever he wants. The women's names are De'mecaline and Mecca. She came across a lot of money when her mother died, and now my husband is driving a new Cadillac Escalade. He is driving all around town and not stopping by our house to find out how the kids are. He also needs to check on me since I am carrying his fifth child.

This woman, Mecca, is going around town, telling folks my husband is divorcing me, and they are going to get married. I even heard she is trying on wedding dresses. Can you believe it? All my husband does is call, call, and call the house. My husband does not visit this house, which is the house we have lived in for ten years. We both picked this house out together. He no longer has conversations with me and the family (neither his immediate family) anymore. Our youngest son has nightmares and cries for his father. Normally, his dad will be home to comfort him. I told him his son cries out for him, and I do not think he cares. When did he become so heartless? Now this woman's friend is harassing me. Presently, I am staying with family members. I need to know what I should do.

Answer 17: Hi, Diane. Your husband does not have any mental defects. He is no different than a woman getting a sugar daddy to provide for her needs. He is finally living a life of what he wants. Diane, your husband has been feeling like he would never pull himself out of the hole of children after children after children and then dealing with a wife. He does not have enough income to live comfortably and, on top of that, to be able to get some of his wants. He was so tired of sacrificing for everyone else.

This is what happened: It was a typical night out at a sports bar. He is drinking a beer at the bar. He is feeling like he can breathe before going home. An anomalous person offers to buy him another beer, and he accepts. Next, came conversation with the woman who bought the beer. Then laughter and more beers. She kept stroking his ego which he had not had from you in years. In the months ahead they meet on his lunch break. She is always bearing gifts, and your husband feels like a kid in a video store with free games galore. He is late from work every day because he stops to see her on his way home. She talks about her hopes and wishes that include being with your husband.

This woman comes into the money after her father died from a terrible accident. Mecca was the beneficiary on her dad's insurance policy. Mecca told your husband about the lucky break and buys him an Escalade in her name to entice your husband. She promises to transfer the title into your husband's name as soon as he gets his divorce from you. He could drive it only if he moves out of the house since he said he felt unhappy and trapped. She did that to get him out of your house and into hers.

So he is driving this big-time vehicle, feeling like a big shot, then along comes watches and new clothes. He looks and feels like the man he has been secretly wanting to look and feel like for a long time. He got all these things without selling drugs and putting his life in jeopardy. I am giving you some insight on how this man of yours has been feeling with every dime he made going to bills, and he barely has enough for beer.

Yes, she is the goose laying the golden eggs, and he likes it. He is so sidetracked to the point that he cannot think straight. He is also ashamed that he is not seeing his boys. He cannot explain his actions of leaving you and how to handle some of the talks his sons have heard in the street. I want to say when the money runs out, he will be back home. He got a taste of the good life and will be trying to convince this woman to help him start up a business so he doesn't have to work hard and wait on a paycheck.

All in all, the new baby will probably be three when he comes back—only if you don't fall in love with this other man that you have been talking and texting too. Time will tell. I don't see you willing to give him a divorce. In the meantime, you may want to apply for a legal separation so you can get some support for you and your children. Your county can give you instructions on how to file. Good luck.

Shift tools 17: Join your county women and parent-support group. Parenting lessons. Reinvent yourself with a career that interests you. Look for mentoring programs to help support the minds of your boys.

Affirmation 17: I am standing strong in the knowledge that I am an excellent parent to my children in any crisis. I am the role model to keep my children safe and secure.

Issue 18: Life or Death—My Mother

Asked Me about Life or Death

My mother claims she saw three women hanging out of an SUV window and swinging a pair of men's boxers, and one woman was saying, "I f——k your man last night. He was doing me real good in my bed." They were laughing and drove off. My mother and I look incredibly alike. She is young-looking. I suspect that B——ches thought she was me. The women said more slurs, according to my mom, and she cannot stand my boyfriend anyway. My mom started a major feud in my home with my boyfriend and I. Then it got physical. My boyfriend tells me my mother interferes too much, and she needs to get her own man. What should I do?

Answer 18: Your boyfriend has a personal secret philosophy, and you may have heard it in some form. He feels he is not married to any woman, and it is not cheating until marriage vows are given in front of the eyes of God, but if spoken, then it is cheating. Exclusive relationships do not count in your boyfriend's eyes. Since he tore up your reputation, the women in his life want to run you off from your so-called man because many of the women that he recently slept with cannot believe he lives with the likes of you, so there is a full-fledged attack on you, Miss Lady.

Respect is out of the window, and your mother sees that you are not being treated with respect. Why can't you see it? Leave your boyfriend; he cannot and will not respect you or any other woman. Yes, he came a long way because of you. Still, he doesn't respect you. Your man does not value you or the relationship. He has called you a jump off. Now, come on. I know he said something to this effect to you in your face. Your mom busted your man, and he's still going to get away with it.

Shift tools 18: See your worth and get back into the interest you had before you got into a relationship with him. You had some cool dreams, and they can come to fruition when you start back investing in you. Look for people who can help you with this venture. LinkedIn could surprise you.

Affirmation 18: I am in a seat of protective love and support with the love of my life, and he treasures and values me.

INSIGHT WITHOUT CHANGE IS MEANINGLESS

Issue 19

My daughter is eighteen, and my son is in the tenth grade I cannot wait until my son graduates from high school. I want out of my marriage now. My marriage has been over years ago. My husband and I do not have anything in common. I am bored with him. Please do not get me wrong; my husband is a good man and a good father. He is devoted to his kids, but they are growing up.

I am not a schoolgirl that needs a sweater for school; I need more than that from a man. I want love and passion from my man that makes me feel like I am alive. This is not what I am going to keep settling for just so the neighbors can look at us as an ideal family. I am over that. Am I supposed to be married for the rest of my life without sex? I don't think so. Quite a few men have been approaching me, and I honor my vows, but now I want to sever them. My husband is trying to keep his business afloat, and I just got elected to be the CFO. I should be happy, but I am growing more and more distant. Ms. Dorothea, what am I supposed to do with a loveless marriage?

Answer 19: Yes, yes, it is natural for individuals that have been together as long as you two have to naturally get cabin fever and be ready to peel off the dusty labels and live life to the fullest. You feel as though life is passing you by, and you are tired of being a spectator in your own life.

All these commercial advertisements of K-Y Jelly sexual ads, Twister, and the "Yours and Mine" intimate gels/creams are everywhere. You feel like a revolution had taken the place of couples. You barely have time to rest in your bed because you stay up late during the night, looking at spreadsheets all night long then falling asleep at his desk. I know this must be frustrating. More and more women in their forties are increasingly being ignited. You are in your high sexual peak, and you feel like a parade is passing you by because the twister is blowing people's mind while you want your mind blown as well. I know you didn't sign up for a passionless marriage.

At the time of your vows, you had no idea life would get in the way, causing some distractions while climbing the ladder to the top. In the midst of your husband trying to keep his business afloat, I feel you became disconnected with him, and that is where communication needs to come back in to the marriage. This is not a time to grow shy to tell your husband what you are missing.

In your conversation with your husband, take him down memory lane. Real communication, not exasperated anger and frustration, an honest communication starts off with the question, "Do you remember when you were hot for me? You would skip a day of work for us to stay in bed all day." Take him back down memory lane and have some drinks while you are both are talking.

Of course, timing is everything; so when he is scratching his head and staring off into space, hand him his favorite beverage. You could play some music by Minnie Riperton, and all those frustrations will start to melt. This talk could easily be in a beautiful hotel that has a delicious dinner menu. Dialogue with your man. This is the key. By the way, order the Twister so you both can find out why everyone's hair is blown back stiff. Then use it back-to-back. His business will fall back into place like butter. On the weekend, you are giving the kids money for the movies quite frequently.

Shift tools 19: Breathe in forty times and relax. Purchase Minnie Riperton or listen to two of your favorite songs from your courting days. Order the Twister, buy your husband a new robe and pajamas. Buy yourself two different sexy nightgowns and pack a weekend bag. Breathe.

Affirmation 19: I have it all, and I am enjoying every moment of it as I stay present in love and communication.

Issue 20: Thirty-Four Years in the Making

What do you say to a woman who has been a man's mistress for forty-four years, and the man has been married for forty-six years? My sisters and I were born before their affair. The one thing that happened was, my mom told us about being with this man. He had to leave our mom at times to be with his wife. In the beginning, he was like a stepdad. He was with us more than his own family.

As time moved forward, that changed; his family went through some tough times. Yet instead, he was still with my mother and us girls. The inevitable took place as his family got older, as well as both my mom and us. My siblings were married and divorced like Mom. As our lives transpired, this man would still stop by. He was always married, and my mother was still with him.

I need a new perspective so that my sisters and I can stop repeating this tragic history that we were exposed to. We cannot find a decent man that is single because I feel we are trapped in this sad cycle of being second to another man's family. I want out of this horrible curse. Yes, it feels like a curse, a habitual, never-ending curse of loneliness and pain. Having lonely nights and being alone on significant holidays has become my life. Help me to find my way out of this.

Answer 20: Help you see your way out of this illusion? You see it clearly. You definitely want more for your life than your mother wanted for her life. Your mother's situation has been a test of will and ego. Your mother was sleeping with this woman's husband while she was not fully divorced from your father at the time. They both took too long to get a divorced from each other. Your stepdad went on to marry his longtime girlfriend, which your mother has known since you girls were infants.

It looks like Mom was always second because she was cheating on your father. Her lover was dating this woman before he met your mother, but your mother was hot to trot and full of life at twenty-nine years of age. The man you call Stepdad could not resist your mother. He always wanted her, but she was married. She started having kids, and the spiral of reasons kept delaying what could have been a beautiful life.

The good thing is their relationship has nothing to do with you, so stop observing and keeping notes as though you are looking for lessons to be lonely. The key is to forgive. Let it go. Release and give thanks to God. Pray and know that God is smart enough to know you want to be happy, but that can only come about if you start thinking about all the aspects of your new lover. Imagine how life starts to make you happy, smile, and be proud to stand beside him, and he will appear. Remember what you want and do not disguise it with anyone. "I don't want him to be unfaithful"—don't say what you do not want because that is how you tell God to keep it coming by bringing all your unfaithful men down the pike for you.

Shift tools 20: Release this formula of being with unavailable men. Regenerate your self-esteem with some self-esteem-building classes.

Affirmation 20: Love is my anecdote, and love allows me to have emotionally and physically available men always moving in my direction. It is my divine right to have a significant love of my life, and I give thanks for it now arriving.

INSIGHT WITHOUT CHANGE IS MEANINGLESS

Issue 21: He Cannot Take My Baby

Hi, Ms. Dorothea. I would like your insight on my situation with my soon-to-be-ex-husband. Just because I was born in another country does not give my husband the right to threaten me with deportation. This man I married feels he owns me like property. I did not marry him for a green card, but that is how he treats me. I am so tired of being in this country with such uncertainty all the time.

We have been married for three years, and we have an eighteen-month-old daughter together. She has been my only bright spot in days of dreariness. When I am at work, I feel good and free, but coming home to the verbal abuse has gotten worse since I was relieved of my job two months ago. I just want to go back home and be with my family; I do not like being in America. My life feels like a bust here. There is so much pain here I cannot understand how the people here sustain themselves.

With my husband, love is very much an afterthought; bullying seems to be his mission and pleasure. I made the mistake to tell him I cannot take it anymore, that I am going back home, and he took our daughter out of the house for three days. He said I was not going to kidnap his child and take her to a county that she knows nothing about, plus having her around strangers.

So he told me, "You go, and she will stay here. Go if you want to, but the child is staying in America because she is American." The tears are flowing day and night, and I am trapped here with a man I despise. He is not the overly sweet guy I dated. I don't know where this man came from because if I knew about his behavior, I would have run a long time ago. I thought I met my prince; instead I met my prisoner of pain. He wonders why I will not sleep with him when he beat me down with words. He thinks I am supposed to hop on his private parts to make him feel good when he makes me feel so bad. Tell me, Ms. Dorothea, what should I do? I trust you so much. Give me some answers. Elequia J.

Answer 21: Hello, Elequia J. I feel your pain deeply. Your situation does seem uncomfortable, especially not knowing where your daughter was for those three days of emotional abuse. Your daughter was at his grandmother's home. Your husband's grandmother had words with him about watching the child. She was wondering why the two of you could not watch your own child for those days. Your husband made up some impossible excuse, but the point is, your grandmother-in-law did not call you to find out what was wrong because you did not call her to confide in your difficulty or ask her about your daughter. You did not call any of your in-laws, and they have no idea you are abused this severely.

However, if you record him some of his conversations when talking to you, that is when they will know about the abuse. If you had communicated with his family, at least 30 percent of your difficulty could have been resolved by communication. You not getting along with his mother does not make it better. Anyway, she just does not like you because you are from Africa. You know his mother has a hang-up about Africans living in America. She thinks that it is mighty convenient that Africans can find their way to America. Being free after slavery is over, but nobody knew how to get here fifty to sixty years ago.

Your husband's grandmother was a part of the civil-rights movement. She has become a Christian, filled with all the kindness in the world until it comes to you and your accent. Sometimes all those thoughts she had welled up inside her—constantly fighting tooth and nail for the right to have a drink of water. Now here come the Africans coming over to America,

INSIGHT WITHOUT CHANGE IS MEANINGLESS

where black people had experienced so much trauma, and now their freedoms are good in place.

Really, the problem is that she does not know her lineage and where she descended from. She does not want to know because she is here, and no one came to rescue her great-great-great-great-great-grandfather who was sold as a child straight from Africa, and that is the story she has. I am sure your husband told you some of this when you two were dating.

Your husband's grandmother does care for you because of her great-grandchild, and she does not believe in woman abuse. She would help you in every way she can, if she knew. You can be linked by a lot of women services that will help you. There are so many at your disposal, and each one will help you. Your inner core has to be strengthened, and only you can do this from the inside out. What do you need to feel whole and complete? Because you cannot successfully live by someone else's set of rules. Diminishing who you are to compromise your integrity has been costly, so now is the time to get prepared to enforce the basic rights of your desires without overshadowing others in your household.

Anyway, I see two immigration attorneys who will help you get your green card in spite of you being on the brink of divorce and the mental abuse. You have many people that will speak on your behalf so that you will have a safe haven in the storm. Your husband also has rights, and I see with the court of law on the side of what is best for the child. The two of you will resolve this conflict. Your husband will be shocked that you found an attorney. His threats seem to disappear, and he begins to act civilized when he finds out you can get your papers with very little help from him. I suspect some of that talk of his grandmother planted some deep roots in him, and unconsciously, he acted out a lot of her issues—nothing to do with you.

Shift tools 21: Start the process of sending love to yourself, your husband, and his family. Especially, send love to his mother and grandmother. How do you do this? First, you think back to one of the sweetest, happiest feelings you remember. Now, this could be the birth of your baby, how beautiful she looked with her tiny fingers and toes. Think of how her lips curled when she smiles.

Think about that precious miracle of life you brought forth, or you can use how your husband wowed you at the time of dating. Another gesture is to think of the birth of your daughter. When you feel this feeling in your heart and mind, hold it as if you could bottle it. Hold that thought until it fills your heart. Imagine that marvelous feeling of being a pink cloud of love and joy.

See the cloud is light as a feather, and it will go where ever you direct it to go. Imagine your arms with twenty of these clouds of love. I want you to imagine sending it out to infiltrate your grandmother-in-law, your husband, your ex-boss, your neighbor, all your husband's family, and to those whether you know them or not, and they seem like they need a dose of love to send it out. Sending love really works, and people begin to feel it just like long-distance healing. Practice this daily or several times a day. You will see remnants of your pink clouds working. Remember, the most disdainful person needs more love, not criticism.

Affirmation 21: I am bound by love only. As I shift my thoughts, my world shifts. I feel lighter and move about my life with effortless ease, getting all that I desire because my focus is love first.

Issue 22: Bipolar or What?

Hi, Ms. Dorothea, my name is Trent. I would like to ask a question: why is it when I ignore this woman, she blows up my telephone like an insane person? I give her attention, but I cannot seem to catch up to her. She is always so busy. Tell me why that is.

Answer 22: Well, Trent, you have what I call a dance-away-lover syndrome. She only wants you when she is feeling lonely and unfulfilled. You are giving her the attention to temporary fill that void that is inside her. No one can feel this void because it's so deep from her beating up on herself with a lot of negative self-talk. You cannot begin to fill this void in her, but what you have been doing are temporary fixes.

It has been working; she gets cocky, and all of sudden, she wants to give you her butt to kiss, especially if you say something she doesn't like or doesn't notice when she does something new to herself. This relationship is exhausting. I feel you need to let this one go. I always advise sex after 120 or more days so that dopamine and oxytocin will not grab you to make you feel like you have some obligation to making her happy despite your happiness. I see you recognized her being damaged. She can repair herself, but she has to want to. Nothing outside of her will work except her own will. She believes she is okay.

Shift tools 22: Get back into your athletics; play some racket ball, basketball, and take a look at playing a golf. Write a list of what you are looking for in a significant other, then try online dating on a paying site. You will catch a couple of prime choices in women. Find a really good church home to attend and look into some classes on growing yourself spiritually.

Affirmation 22: My desires are fulfilled with everything that I enjoy in life—love, wonderful conversation, physical fitness, a career that challenges me to grow, and a life of peace, happiness, and real satisfaction. I am truly blessed.

Issue 23: Why Fix It If It Is Not Broken?

Hi, Ms. Dorothea. I do not like feeling pressured. I have been with my girlfriend for three years, and she is talking marriage all the time. I agreed to live together, so why the pressure of marriage? What is the difference? Why marriage? We have been very happy together. I have not seen anybody happy after marriage. Am I wrong, or am I wrong? I am not interested in marriage.

Answer 23: Why are you stringing this woman along? Well, if this is your belief, then you are right. Whatever your belief compiles of within you is your right. Therefore, you are right, but that does not mean your girlfriend had to go for it. It is obvious you love her and care about what she thinks because you would not have agreed to live with her. You need to talk to her and tell her that you do not have any intentions of getting married. Allow her to decide whether she wants to be with you. She was hoping to manipulate you into something that is not going to happen. She can come to her senses and move on or get involved with a man that wants the whole package instead of playing house. The years you guys put into playing house could add up on social security benefits and other kinds of government perks and insurances you have when you retire. I hope you are not under the impression you will not age because, buddy, you certainly will. So play house with someone who does not care about these things. You should break up with your girlfriend and tell her the truth. Stop stringing her along.

Shift tools 23: Go to the retirement homes and ElderCare hospitals to poll how many unmarried men die sick and alone or have waited for their siblings or children (of the unmarried women) to help with them because of their decisions to be a playboy when they were young. They could have taken the time to find the ideal wife and build a life with a wonderful spouse. A wife might have kept them healthier longer than their single lifestyle. A dying, sick player does not look so appealing.

Affirmation 23: I attract my ideal relationship, and we are on the same page. We want the same things, and we think the same way. My ideal is here, and I am grateful for her.

Issue 24: Tired, or Is He Keeping Company with a Pair of Long Legs?

Hi, Ms. Dorothea, this is Eva. My boyfriend drives an eighteen-wheeler truck, and he is on the road more than he is at home. I never questioned what he was doing because we talked all the time until recently. All of a sudden, when I have to call him to find out what's going on, he is a little short with me. I never questioned his whereabouts until now. Lately our rent has been late; before everything was paid beforehand. My boyfriend's job has not changed, neither has his salary. I keep asking the question, "What's going on? Is there someone else?" Am I right to be suspicious, or is he just tired and want a better-paying job, like he is always saying lately? Should I just trust him?

Answer 24: Hi, Eva. Your situation must be making you feel worried and filled with anxiety, but I do see that your boyfriend loves you. He loves you so much he hates disappointing you, and he knows how you get when there is bad news, so he usually tries to avoid giving you bad news.

Well, in this case, he lost a shipment by arriving very late because he was so sleepy and didn't get to his destination on time; hence he was terminated. Your boyfriend has been out looking for work or another trucker's gig, but his last company has put the word out of his lateness. I suspect all those conversations with you when he should have been sleeping has been the problem.

He loves you and is doing his very best to repair the problem, which soon will be fine. I see that he will be back on the road this week. In the meantime, some of the stashes of money you have been putting away (I won't say hiding) should carry the bills for a short while. He is been working on other people's rigs, and these people are always late in paying him.

Shift tools 24: Release the paranoia with some physical activity. Take a spin class at your local gym, or an aerobics class as well that incorporates dance to get you feeling great and to motivate you to raise your vibration, and recognize when someone loves you.

Affirmation 24: I have a loving and wonderful mate because I am loving, and I always receive love throughout each moment of my life.

Issue 25: I Guess It Was Too Close for Comfort

Hi, Ms. Dorothea. I need some advice about a guy that I love. The problem is, he has been a friend of the family for such a long time. He and his wife are in a take-no-prisoner-divorce fight right now. Over these last seven months we have gotten close, but during the previous two weeks, I haven't heard from him. It seems like he is avoiding my calls. What should I do? Is he rekindling with his wife, or has he found somebody else? My mind won't stop racing because I allowed my heart to be penetrated with his love, and I feel he is throwing what we have away. What can I do? Lydia J.

Answer 25: Well, Lydia J., you can allow him to grieve. You gave such incredible comfort to a man who thought he would be losing his mind in regard to a woman he vowed to love and cherish. He does not recognize the woman to whom he said his vows too. Though you came to give him support, he began to feel the vice grips of your help, which felt like a prison of emotions. You were crowding him with the pretense of help, but he has not resolved his present situation.

Now, it was nice that the two of you got something out of this tender moment or moments you had with one another. You have to stop acting like a desperate female and act like a woman that has compassion and not an agenda. Divorces are like funerals; there is a grieving process. No matter what past divorcees may say, it is painful giving your all and losing your efforts to sustain life for love.

Hearing all that he has done for his wife is a form of purging and releasing his pain. It's not supposed to be a checklist of what you may be getting in the future. In fact, there is no future for you with this man. He is planning on relocating to his hometown and taking a job there once all this is done. If you had an agenda to be with this man, you might be disappointed; but if you really care about him, you will find in your heart to understand his decision. To continue this relationship with him will turn him into a spectacle for all to see, and he does not want to be scrutinized by the friends that he and his wife have together. Timing is everything.

Shift tools 25: Seek available men, especially who have been divorced for some time. Breathe deep breaths frequently and release the need to rescue. Seek tips and tricks of the lifestyles of single women seeking loving relationships.

Affirmation 25: I take joy in the fulfillment of love and have an expectancy of preparing for my mentally and emotionally available love for myself.

Issue 26: Sexual Harassment Is the Only Answer

Hi, Ms. Dorothea. I got fired, or laid off, and I think it is because I didn't want to go to bed with my boss. It was getting increasingly difficult to work at this job where I dressed very professionally. I kept getting a barrage of compliments, and it was becoming uncomfortable. I was used to the compliments, so it didn't bother me, but the brushing up against me and speaking so close as though he were going to kiss me was unacceptable. I spoke clearly that I was uncomfortable with his unwelcome behavior and suggested he e-mail me what he wants instead of me coming to his office as often as he would have me. I got fired.

Answer 26: This is very unacceptable, and I hope you have a clear paper trail of your incidents with conversations of your boss. This should go further, and it will stick with valued documentation. You will also need documentation on how well you were doing your job and your interactions with other coworkers while at the workplace.

You cannot allow this to affect your self-esteem, and you can't doubt if you were doing the right thing or not. Never let your personal space to be taken away from you. You may have to report this with the federal Equal Employment Opportunity Commission (EEOC) at www.eeoc.gov or 1-800-669-4000 and/or your state's fair employment agency, or look it up at http://www.equalrights.org/legal-help/know-your-rights/sexual-harassment-at-work/#sthash. You must take back your power.

Shift tools 26: Self-esteem work.

Affirmation 26: I am a strong, confident individual, and I have justice on my side. I release any fear or doubt trying to show up in my life. I am free and happy. This is my life, and what I want is happening in wonderful ways.

Issue 27: I Want What I Want—

It's What Makes Me Happy

Hi, Ms. Dorothea. I want this guy; he is tall, sexy, good-looking, and is a Libra—my ideal match. Often we flirt with each other at work. He has not asked me out yet. I hope he is single. In passing I noticed he is very sociable with the people in the office. Yes, it has been rumored that he was in a relationship with one of the ladies here at work.

However, it appears the two of them try not to give eye contact with one another. Our department went out for happy hour, and I struck up a conversation with him. By the way, his name is Larry. The conversation was good, and I found out that he is a single man that lives alone. I live alone as well. We both are hoping the company gives out raises this year. Mainly our conversation was small talk about the drinks he likes, as well as the fact people cannot smoke in the building at work anymore. I do know he hates smokers, and that's about it.

Answer 27: Larry is a nice, kind fellow and a good friend with the lady at your job. She is a confidant that holds his secrets. My dear, Larry is gay and is not interested in you.

Shift tools 27: Mirror work is to work out the desperation of loneliness. Feel love in every part of your being.

Affirmation 27: I attract men that are interested in me and my well-being. The male for me is here and enjoys a life of love, laughter, and commitment.

Issue 28: If You're Not Happy, Leave

I am so pissed and hurt that I was lied to. This man at my job that I have seen for several months lied to me about his relationship status. I have been going to his place for months. It looked like any bachelor home; there was no sign of a woman because every chance I got, I checked. This guy had the nerve to start talking about planning a future. We talked about living together, meeting each other's family, and moving forward like in a regular relationship. Now he is telling me him and his wife are talking about getting back together. He keeps insisting that he told me he was married. Even if that was the case, why was he talking about the future and meeting my folks over the holidays?

Answer 28: Okay, what's done is done, and you can't go back in time and retrieve those moments you had together. It is time to move forward by releasing the relationship but, more importantly, to release your guilt. I can clearly see this relationship went against your moral fiber.

Shift tools 28: How to release guilt—shift energy not to attract unavailable men. (You do not attract what you want; you attract who you are.)

Affirmation 28: I attract what I genuinely desire; exclusivity and unconditional love. I attract this because I give this, and I honor myself. I cannot attract what does not honor me.

Issue 29: My Wife Needs to Get a Life

My wife wants to put our daughter in beauty pageants, which I feel is very exploitive; I never can get Jon Benet Ramsey out of my mind. My wife's beauty-pageant days are long over, and I keep telling her not to live her dreams through our daughter. I remember my mother was strict with my sisters. In my opinion, my mother was paranoid about men giving too much attention to my sisters, so she did not allow them to sit on my uncles' or any male neighbor's laps. I always noticed that my sisters sat on my dad's lap, which wasn't noticeable growing up. Then years later all the speculation surrounding the little girl's death of Jon Benet Ramsey.

Answer 29: It is true your wife wants a little queen for herself. She also wants to have some form of accomplishment and acknowledgment, which raising the first-place winner to a queen speaks volumes to her. This experience will mean lots of media exposure, travel, interviews, money, Reality TV (she's hoping), and bragging rights. She wants your baby to be the next Honey Boo-Boo; she asks herself, Why not?

I know you don't want to think about what all the anonymous, sick people are doing, but God knows what your daughter's likely to become; this could be very disturbing to you. Although, your daughter will be safe. Other than that, you and your wife need reality counseling. With counseling, your wife will be able to come down to earth and realize she is living through her daughter's life. You need to be more understanding with your wife even if you don't agree; try to understand her viewpoint. I know you have the ability to look at both sides of an issue.

Shift tools 29: Deep breathing for five minutes. Neck and shoulder rolls loosen up all that stored-up tension. Read my book of prayers and affirmations. Then read the "12 Steps to Forgiveness" by Paul Ferrini.

Affirmation 29: I am a loving, supportive husband and father. My family and I come together as a cohesive fit. I allow a change in my life, and the changes always turn into opportunities for the highest and best good for all concerned.

Issue 30: I'm out!

Hi, Ms. Dorothea, how are you? I would like to start out by saying, you are amazing! You have helped me numerous times that gave me an excellent new perspective on my career and growth in myself. I have done all the homework you outlined, all the self-help work, and I even went to a retreat or two. I feel like I am becoming the best person I can be.

Although my husband is still a jerk, jerk, jerk, jerk in that order, which sometimes I think I must be a jerk as well because I married him. I'm ready to leave this marriage; I've been prepared to leave this marriage for a while. Why am I still in this marriage? My husband is the laziest man in the world. He works, but that's all he does. He won't interact with his children nor with his own family. I can't get him to cut the lawn or fix a crack in the counter of the kitchen with grout. He won't wrench a pipe or suck out a clog; any repairs in this house I must call a "honey do" man for my upkeep. What good is the one I have?

Well, I have come to the conclusion, if he can't do anything in this house, I can't lift my legs in the bedroom either. Frankly, I do not want him to brush up against me anyway. Dorothea, this is horrible to say, but he makes my skin crawl. How do I handle this and get out without raising holy hell? The money he gives me can contribute to a college fund or child support whatever. I'm out.

Answer 30: I am doing well, thank you for asking. Well, Miss Lady, as I am reading this letter, a few bullet points are left out.

Bullet point number 1: You wanted a man who could provide for you, love his home, and stay home, which this man does. He spends a lot of time in the den, watching various games. Bullet point number 2: You bullied your way into a proposal through ultimatums. You said you were going to leave your husband earlier because you were not completely happy with him. However, you did not want to throw away all those years you have invested in this man. Bullet point number 3: He barely got off the couch when you were dating. Now you are upset that he doesn't get off the couch, and you are married.

I'm confused on why you are raising holy hell with the whole house, making everyone uncomfortable in the home. Why go to retreats and do self-help work if your anger takes over and turns you into a beast? Your husband cannot always be the catalyst for your frustrations. What is eating you? I think I know; you started a little more despairing by comparing your life to girlfriends, coworkers and their spouses, probably television shows and their pretend spouses. You know if you start to compare, eventually despair sets in. Decide to stay or leave, but do not tear up the house with your emotional despair.

Shift tools 30: Breathe in deep for twenty minutes. Anger release exercise; take an imaginary gold balloon and blow all your worries, concerns, and frustrations into it. Tie it up and say, "I release this discomfort so I can be free to live my life free." Also get your chakras cleared and balanced. Reiki and/or Pranic Healing is needed. Cleanse and clear your aura. Go to a retreat that is not sponsored by some weekend self-help warriors.

Affirmation 30: I have a life of many rewards that I recognize. The joy of life has given me wonderful opportunities in love, sharing and speaking the positive accomplishments of others while raising the vibration of love for all concerned.

Issue 31: I Like to Drink, So What's the Big Deal?

I am not hurting anyone. My boyfriend gets on my last nerve, and I am really good to him. My boyfriend is on long-term disability with limited income. The money does not matter to me because I love him for him. When my boyfriend's funds are short, I am the person that kept his phone and cable turned on. I gave him a surprise birthday party, paid to get some repairs done on his home (painting the walls) and getting the plumbing done in his home (bathroom). So he rewards me by cussing me out and telling everybody I drink too much. He has a foul tongue, and I don't say much about the words that are spoken toward me.

When I express to him I want some attention and he doesn't give it to me, I tell him that he doesn't do anything for me. Then he tells me I can go back across town to go home if I don't like it. So that is exactly what I did: I picked up my sh——t and went back home. After a few days he calls me back-to-back, back-to-back nonstop like a crazy person. Then he wants to get married and talking about buying another place for the two of us. How is he going to do this when he doesn't ever have any money to keep his damn cable on? I know this, but I still run back over there for some stupid flowery words and some ten-minute man sex. why? I know why—because I don't have anybody else.

Answer 31: So you are sad that you knew the answer. This is also because you had many disappointing relationships with men in the past, including this one in the present, and the cycle continues. Do you feel the cycle is just continuing? During your whole adult life, you don't know how it should feel to have a wonderful, loving man who is considerate of you and your feelings.

I feel like you are not considerate and caring about your own feelings. All you know how to do is put everyone first. How would you like them to act? You are the person that perpetuated the selfish attitude by giving them permission to be selfish and not to think of you. When you put the needs of everyone else before yours, you bitch about it. Then you want to complain to everyone and wonder why you keep being taken advantage of over and over, year after year with your own family, children, friends, and lovers.

Come on, when is this going to stop? C'mon, this behavior has to stop! You are going to have to take the risk by putting your own needs first. For you to do that, you will need to sit down in a quiet place to figure out what your needs are. *Baby*, you will be in pain for the rest of your life if you stay on this locomotive. You cannot go back to the first man in your life, wishing the past to change.

It feels like you still want the warmth and attention from your dad. Unfortunately, that is not the case. You have to look at the woman in the mirror because she is the only person that can change this. What is it that you want? Love? How does one give love to themselves? You must first start by liking what you see in the mirror. Stop talking about plastic surgery. Like the person that you are right now. Look into the bathroom mirror into your own eyes and love the reflection you see before you. Then take off the layers of clothing you are wearing. This is the time to start loving every piece of that body of yours. *Eh*, I don't want to hear it. Take it off! There are individuals who no longer have their limbs or parts of their body that value themselves more than you. C'mon, love your appearance.

Shift tools 31: Imagine you are on a plane. The plane is having problems and appears to be going down. The oxygen mask has dropped from the ceiling, and panic is at the severe high. What are you going to do? You are going to oxygenate yourself first and then get calm to see who you can help next. This exercise is about *you* putting your needs first.

Affirmation 31: I put myself first. It is okay to put myself first because I can take care of me. I will be productive in the world and keep myself in good spirits. It will be my choice to provide assistance to someone else and not assisting out of desperation. Love is given to me freely, and love recognizes me for who I am—love.

Issue 32: His Kids Are Running and Ruining Our Relationship

Hi, Ms. Dorothea. I am tired of playing second fiddle to my man's kids. They come over to the house every other weekend. My so-called man and I don't see one another. Basically, we only see each other two weekends a month, but he is with me and my kids throughout the week. His excuse is he doesn't want to interrupt his routine with kids. The kid's mother is in a serious relationship, so he feels they are being alienated at times. He also feels him giving them sole exclusivity to him will help his kids handle life better.

My boyfriend, Donald, wants me to be patient with him. He says he will slowly incorporate my kids and me into their lives. Well, it has been two years almost three, and I am starting to wonder if I really have a boyfriend. I feel that part of his life with his kids is off limits, and heaven forbid they want Daddy (Donald) to take them somewhere during the week. I am sitting around, waiting on his call or his returns. The summers are worst; I only get to see him if he leaves the kids with his mother or sister since he has the kids during the summer. I love him, but I love myself more to be dealing with this type of behavior, which is keeping myself in waiting or subservient mode. Why am I waiting?

Answer 32: Hope keeps you waiting for Donald to come around. You feel if you do everything to make him feel comfortable and supported, he will see the merit in you and the relationship. He is a man of sound principals and passion when the two of you are alone.

The truth is, you are feeling ignored by Donald. You are becoming a woman of convenience. Why wait as the months turn into years and progress has only been one-sided despite the conversations the two of you had with one another night after night and day after day? You were asked to have patience despite the signs all around you that say a loving companion, as you witnessed loving couples, seems to be in abundance and is stranger than ever. Almost three years these children are growing older, as well as your children.

A way of life has been set, and your gut feeling is telling you this will not be a combined family unit. Whatsoever his kids want is what goes; you are not running anything. You have a choice to make, whether to keep allowing your years to be eaten up like Pac-Man or find a responsible new mate that cherishes you and shares his life with you.

Shift tools 32: Aerobic class to exert some of that pent-up energy.

Affirmation 32: I have a wonderful life, combined with my children, my man's children, and family. We have a beautiful, cohesive family unit of love. I send out love, and it returns like a boomerang.

Issue 33: I Think My Girl Is Still Sleeping with Her Kid's Father

I can never seem to visit her when she is expecting the kid's father to pick up the children or to drop off money to the children. When I met my little shorty, it didn't matter to me that she had three kids. She was once married to their father, but now she is divorced. I have two kids of my own. I have never been married, so I can't trip, you know, but I am feeling her. I help my girl with whatever she needs because I do consider myself a real man.

Don't get me wrong, Ms. Dorothea, I take care of my own kids as well and pick them up from time to time when their mother is not acting whack or tripping on some sh——t. Well, you know what I mean. Anyway, yo dude be coming by the house too often when we don't always have time to chill. I need to know what's up for real though. I need to know, should I bounce, or hang in there? J. Lover

Answer 33: I understand where you are coming from, J. Lover, but what you don't understand is that one of her kids complained about you yelling at him. You also lock the door when you and their mommy are in the room together. That is the reason why the kids' father is coming around more. He loves his kids, and he doesn't want to catch a case knocking you out about his kids. He warned the kid's mom about the complaint, and she hasn't said anything to you.

I am beginning to believe she likes him coming around because she longs to be a family again. He was a good provider, but a little stuffy or square or boring, so she thought. I feel she wants some boring, which brings her some consistency. Let me just say this, your days are numbered.

Shift tools 33: Read the book "The Five Love Languages." It will help you in the future to understand women. Shivery is not a dirty word. Bring something for the kids when you visit and for your girl. Stop being so empty-handed because you're making her ex look good.

Affirmation 33: I will treat women like the queens that they deserve to be, and I attract queens because I am King Quality.

Issue 34: Should I Tell My Mother?

Should I tell my mother her boyfriend is trying to take me out and get with me sexually? I am afraid she won't believe me.

Answer 34: Yes, you should tell your mother, but before you do, get a few video recordings/audio recordings of your mother's boyfriend on your phone without him knowing it. Download it to your computer and e-mail the recording to yourself. When you have this meeting with your mother, tell her and then show her the evidence. You may want to tell your grandmother and your aunt that is close to you. Your aunt has been wondering about your mood changes.

It's imperative that you get this evidence without any coercion on your part. Allow things to happen naturally. Your extended family will give moral support to you because your mother still may just talk to her boyfriend and try to clear it up with, "It was just a misunderstanding," instead of getting rid of him. If that is the case, you will have to move in with an extended family because there will be a rape. If your mom doesn't believe you, tell anybody—teacher, church clergy, a neighbor, a parent of a friend, and worst-case scenario call 1-888-PREVENT (1-888-773-8368). Stop it now. Your mother will believe that, for you to go to all this trouble, something must have happened.

Shift tools 34: You have nothing to be guilty about. Find a prayer line with the Spiritual Living Center and see if you could join a teen group at a spiritual living center.

Affirmation 34: I am well within my rights to keep my innocence intact, and I will not back down when my personal space is invaded. I have the support of the universe and all the powers that be keeping me safe.

Issue 35: Last Year of Law School

Hi, Ms. Dorothea. I am in my last year of law school, and I just found out I am pregnant. I want to tell my husband, but other days I do not want to tell him. He has wanted a child for quite some time. I don't want to tell him because he has not been my advocate in this law-school venture, which he continues to say I forced down his throat rather than start a family.

This is such a huge accomplishment for me, which I think in the long run will help us when we eventually decide together to start having a family. My husband doesn't shine when I share my grades with him, and he barely looks interested each time my grades come in. If I tell my husband I got another "A," he seems to sulk harder, as though he was expecting me to quit any day. I refuse to drop out, and I don't want to lose my marriage.

Sundays are the worst; even though I need to study, I still attend church and Sunday dinners at his parents' home. It's a ritual, and his parents, mainly his mother, keeps hinting about our age and asking when their grandchild is coming. Lord, give me strength because I don't want to disrespect them, but I do feel like kicking my husband under the table because he says absolutely nothing when his mother whines about a grandchild. As it seems as if this conversation was rehearsed. My husband talks to his mother every day more than I talk to mine. All I want to do is finish law school, find a high position, and be a wife to my husband, which should not be hard.

Answer to 35: Congratulations on such a momentous accomplishment. You should be so proud of yourself. I see you believe in self-sabotage because attending church is all well, and it helps to uplift your week. However, to participate in Sunday dinners only to feel deflated takes away the purpose of going to church in the midst of trying to accomplish such a wonderful task.

This is your last year; you may have to excuse yourself from some of those Sunday dinners and get to your dining-room table to study. I see your husband will bring you a plate every time, and when you do attend the Sunday dinner, there will not be any hints as there were in the past for fear of seeing her son hurt without you by his side. The topic will take on an interest in your accomplishments and on how your mother and father-in-law may need you once you become an attorney.

Shift tools 35: Shift perspective and appreciate your accomplishments by completing school guilt-free. Stay proud of yourself. Keep yourself motivated by prayer work and reading prayer books before retiring for bed and upon waking to start your day.

Affirmation 35: My life is complete and fulfilled. Love permeates my home and in all that I do.

Issue 36: Fifty and Waiting

I have not been married, and I am still waiting for Ms. Right so that I can make her Mrs. Wright. I meet quite a few women who want to be on the Wright team, but they didn't make the cut, or the women just didn't have what it takes to stand the test of time. When is this woman going to arrive in my life? My children want me to have a wife because they don't want to take care of me when I get old. Where's my wife? I am physically fit. Everybody pretty much makes the mistake that I'm around thirty-five. TJ Wright

Answer 36: Mr. Wright, the truth is, you have been scared of relationships, but not intimate encounters. What I mean by that is failed relationships. You assume the inevitable would happen to you because of all the failures that you have been privy to know. The tabloids are not any better at their failures and money. It looks like you did some research on your own family relationships, and there are not too many success stories with them either.

In addition to the work part of relationships, yes, it takes work to grow a relationship, and it seemed harder than any venture capital investment, which you do in your work. Once the honeymoon phase of a relationship is over, the real action takes place; personalities begin to dance the dance of compatibility. With each step a red flag shines brightly, almost too bright to bare. When the dance seems to be entirely out of step, you jump ship without any warning to the female that's involved.

Shift tools 36: Join a radical forgiveness group or an intimate discussion group on how to build love. Join a steppers dance group and/or join a meditation group to learn how to listen to your higher self.

Affirmation 36: I am full of love and understanding. Love and understanding are part of my natural life. I attract like a boomerang—a woman who is full of love and understanding. My life is like no other. All modes of discontent, failure and powerlessness are now and forever broken in my chain of relationships

Issue 37: Turn Lemons into Lemonade, I Always Say

I just broke up with my boyfriend because for a while now he was not paying enough attention to me. I was talking to him about the cake his mother wanted for her event. I kept talking and talking and got no response from him. Then I noticed he was looking at the women in the produce section of the grocery store. I was in the produce section too, squeezing some tomatoes.

INSIGHT WITHOUT CHANGE IS MEANINGLESS

When I noticed he was looking at the woman, I picked up a tomato and threw it at him, hitting him in the square of his bald head. He was pretending to pick up some lemons when I threw the tomato at him. Needless to say, he was embarrassed so much that he walked out of the store and drove home. I had to catch a cab home with my lemons for his mother's lemon pound cake and cheesecake. He won't speak to me or respond to why he felt the need to disrespect me staring at that woman while I was less than two feet from him. He has not responded to the e-mail, text and voice message I left for him. I am getting ready to put the question, "Is this relationship over? Is this how you want our relationship to end?" in a card and mail it to him. I just need an answer, and I will be done. It will be closure for me.

Answer 37: Square in his bald head in front of a store full of customers, a wet tomato squished down the back of his neck, and he drove off without you…that's all (you're lucky). I know your antics were the talk around the dinner table or in traffic on the way home; check YouTube—you might be on it. So take pleasure that when he cools off, he will respond. It's not over yet. If you are pushing for a breakup, you are on the right track. Lovingly, you could have handled that a better way.

By walking and standing next to him and saying, "Don't stare. I got her number for you," (facetiously) with a written note in your hand to give to him that says, "If you don't put your damn eyes back in your head, I know something wet will be on you, and it's not my panties." In your other hand place a squashed tomato in his hand and walk away to continue with your produce shopping; that way, nobody is the wiser. Now, with all that drama I just described above, you can't figure out why he is not talking to you?

Shift tools 37: Behavior-management courses, a course in miracle lesson, and mirror work, practicing loving yourself in a full-length mirror. Forgiveness classes. Read a prayer book of your choice. ('Cause you need Jesus, LOL.)

Affirmation 37: I am deserving of devoted and caring love. I am caring, devoted, and it returns to me multiplied abundantly. Love and tenderness are the cornerstones of my relationship, and I always display such tenderness.

Issue 38: Who Says Long-Distance Dating

Brings Heartache? Well, They Were Right

Hi, Ms. Dorothea, this is Camille again. Ache, ache, ache, and my heart is doing flip-flops over my long-distance romance. Last night my fiancé said he was having dinner with friends. When I called him three hours later, he said he was headed home, but when I called, he was not at home.

The reason why I know this is because he didn't answer his landline nor his cell phone. I called the police after I could not reach him for six hours. The police officer responded to my call and told me there was no one home when he knocked.

Mysteriously he arrived as the police were about to leave, and I was on the phone when the police questioned him, asking if he lived here, and I could hear him answer. The police said to me, "Call him. he is now home." My fiancé was so pissed, but I was more pissed too. I thought he was hurt or sick or something. This was out of character for him, and he said he was with a friend without elaborating on where he was at, which he normally does.

Answer 38: Camille, he is embarrassed, furious, and not explaining that his friend was someone from his past. When he met with his friend, their conversation went over time. They went down memory lane and caught up on what was going on in their personal life. He didn't want to explain to you why he didn't answer your call because it would create a barrage of inquisition of questions, and he was not in the mood for that. Yes, she knows he has a fiancé out of town. He was tempted to call her back to tell her he broke up with you, but he got a beer and went to bed.

Shift tools 38: Breathe belly deep fifty times.

Affirmation 38: I attract safe, secure, and satisfying relationships.

Issue 39: Where the Hell Is Romance in this Text

Messaging, Facebook, and Tweeting Phenomenon?

I've been single for about ten years. I have been trying to find a decent man to be with. It's next to impossible, and even more so, a man that's not lying about some woman stashed somewhere or five to fifty kids all around the city. I want one good guy. Is that too hard to ask for and not attached with the mental, emotional, and physical baggage of his past?

Answer 39: Romance is alive and well. It is within the person who desires it. We all carry an atmosphere of our desires and wants within. Romance should be an inside job wrapped with the atmosphere of you because you will notice the men you are attracted to will bring wine or flowers or something, not to be empty-handed unless you are attracting men going through a midlife crisis.

They are bringing a condom instead of flowers to keep from being empty-handed. Well, then we know what type of party that is. What are you settling for? Yes, this is an age of advancements in dating, but it doesn't mean you will attract some young kid who is language deficient and tactile-infused. Now you will attract someone who is caught up in the times of this millennium that still look for values in his life partner that mirrors his. He will be carrying that atmosphere the same as you to attract you. I hope you understand what I am trying to convey.

Shift tools 39: Watch romantic movies to raise romantic vibrations within yourself.

Affirmation 39: I attract many romantic suitors for dating, and I found my wonderful life partner because of my many romantic interests.

Issue 40: Alone, Sacrifice, Work, and Date?

Hi, Ms. Dorothea. I still have a hard time dating while I am raising my two girls. It is hard for a single mother to work and help with homework, get the girls ready for school, keep their level of activities up, and teach them to be respectable to one another in the society. How do I become a good role model for my daughters while dating a man that is not their father? Most importantly, how do I learn to trust men around my precious girls? I believe man doesn't care about f——king another man's daughter as long as it didn't come from their loins and sometimes if it did. When can I release the fear that all men are not predators and have moral values? I don't want to be alone until my girls are eighteen-plus years of age. I don't want to be alone. My children deserve to see what a healthy relationship looks like.

Answer 40: It's called a babysitter. Life is not meant to be so complicated, so stop complicating it. You buy everything else you want, look for a sitter.

Shift tools 40: Go to Care.com and pick out the best person to meet the needs of you and your daughters. Then you hire that person while you go out on some dates.

INSIGHT WITHOUT CHANGE IS MEANINGLESS

Affirmation 40: I live my life to the fullest being a role model to my girls. Life has wonderful surprises for me, and I embrace them all with love, and I get love in return.

Issue 41: I Would Never Have Believed It

Hey, Ms. Dorothea. My buddy said to me that I should give you a try. You helped him in a big way and saved his life, plus his relationship. He is forever grateful to you. I am wondering what you could do for me. I said to my buddy if you can help get him out of what I thought was an impossible ordeal (can we say Al Grits Green), then I got to give you a try because my buddy was—heh, heh, heh—doing some wild stuff.

Okay, I am sixty years old, divorced, and all my kids are grown. I have been dating this woman, Lorraine, for about five years now, and she is a lovely lady. I went out one night about one year ago and met this other young lady who was down for fun with no strings attached. I must admit she had my nose wide open to the point Lorraine was about to call it quits, and she literally hit me upside my head with a towel. Well, four months ago, the trick called me up, saying she is pregnant and it's mine, so she said. I about had a coronary right there in the middle of the street. All these cars were honking their horns at me, giving me the finger. I am too old to be a daddy, and I don't remember ever not using a condom. Help me out of this jam, Ms. Dorothea, please!

Answer 41: It's your baby. She was doing so many tricks, sitting on you like a chair and wiggling her butt for you while taking that condom off. She was having so much sex with you because she wants some of that pension you been bragging about. When that baby comes, you'll be sixty-one years old and no Lorraine in sight. She told you to get rid of your no-good friend, which you did not; if you had listened, this situation would have never occurred.

If you are retired, the judge is lenient toward you. Your child support payment will not be as much, especially if you have an attorney helping you with your case against her. There is a slim chance it's not yours because she has a boyfriend, but you make a whole lot more than the young boyfriend. Tell Lorraine.

Shift tools 41: Come to terms with your action.

Affirmation 41: I recognize love when it is in front of me, and I am grateful for Lorraine.

Issue 42: Hell on Wheels

I married a man with three daughters and a cat. The whole time I was dating him I was not allergic to his cat's fur, but all of the sudden I find myself allergic to his cat and his daughters'. It's amazing how much disrespect I get. My husband has no clue that he's raising monsters in the flesh; they steal my clothing and lie about it. I am miserable, and I cannot continue living with this much level of disrespect. My husband is never around to hear how disrespectful his girls are to me. You should hear some of the things that come flying out of their filthy mouths.

Answer 42: Get a nanny cam, smart cam, or a camera to record their butts for your husband's viewing pleasure when they are misbehaving. The disrespect will stop immediately. The cat is taking a beating on your immune system, making you feel miserable. Get some allergy shots while you are recording the girls, and all this will go away.

Shift tools 42: Shift your energy to another perspective. Do not look at this situation as a victim; be empowered and purchase a nanny cam to rescue you.

Affirmation 42: My home is a place of sanctuary. I stand firm in the love I have for my husband and take the role as the heart of this home.

Issue 43

I am feeling hopeless and alone. The love of my life, or what I thought was the love of my life, has gotten married. I am looking for a new love, but I don't know why I haven't found love yet. Is it because I don't want to be with anyone other than him? What can I do?

Answer 43: Self-worth is the answer. When you focus of the measure of your own self-worth, that's when you can be all that you can be, instead of acting as this is the only man who found you remotely interesting enough to be with you or sleep with you. Snap out of it! He was showing you a lot of red flags, but you didn't pay attention to him. He gave you a lot of broken promises while he was missing in action. How are you forgetting all the late-night evenings alone and the pain you suffered? Are you surprised he was with someone else after so many broken dates? C'mon, you are worthy of so much more than problems. I am waiting for you to see it.

Shift tools 43: Self-esteem classes, radical forgiveness classes.

Affirmation 43: I attract worthy love in my life because I am the epitome of love.

Issue 44: I Am Not as Happy as I Was Three Years Ago

My boyfriend has been out of work for about two and a half years and counting because he quit his job to reinvent himself. He wanted to make more money, so he found a sales job, which ripped him off since he has no sales experience. I felt this was the perfect time for him to visit his family and take care of some loose ends. Instead, he started hanging out late with his friends, trying to get into the music industry at forty-six years of age; he is starstruck at my expense. I am tire—well, exhausted—because we have been together 3.5 years, and he could never really afford the expenses in his apartment. Everything was late, such as his rent, car note, water bill, utilities, everything.

The money he worked for was never enough to cover his expenses. He lived with a roommate and decided to move on his own for privacy. I met him when he was in his place six months ago into our relationship, not knowing the gas would be cut off soon.

Often he would stay with me to save his money until he got enough money to turn back on the gas. Next thing you know, something else would be turned off, and he can't pay the rent or his car insurance, and he hasn't paid his car note in six months. My boyfriend has the nerve to have this king attitude and wanting to be catered to just because he had a job that paid enough to get a postage stamp. I feel as though he should help out more and do whatever it takes to live to be comfortable in the home we live in together, but all he does is complain to no end.

I have broken up with him ten times, but we're still together. He is holding onto me like I am a life preserver in the water while the *Titanic* in the background is sinking. I am not saying he isn't a good man because he is, for somebody else. We've outgrown our time together. I don't have trouble saying what's on my mind, but it is hard for me to put a man out with nowhere to go. I paid for a one-way ticket so he could visit his family back east. He was gone for about three months.

During the time he was away, he contacted my son to ask him to come to visit him for the holidays, but he actually wanted the two of us to come. I had work to do, so I did not go. Yet instead I stupidly sent my son to visit him, knowing deep inside me his plan was to come back home with my son. To make a long story short, he is back living with me with a little-better attitude, still not working and claiming he's looking for work.

When he was back east with his family, he had four interviews. Since he's been back, he hasn't had any (except for those sales gigs). I know his real job is back east. How do I get him out of my house and back east with his family for good? Why can't he stay with any of his friends in the city where we live? In the meantime, he is broke, and his pride is the size of a football field. His friends do not want him to stay with them because he's broke. I did it in the past by allowing people to stay with me until they are able to get back on their feet. Those people I have helped did get back on their feet, except this one, my boyfriend.

At this time in my life, I feel like I do not want to live with another soul for a very long time unless they are doing far more superior than I am. This relationship has shifted me, and what I am looking for is my sanity. Before the recession, I didn't mind helping anyone and I still do to some degree. I really do not mind helping others, but there are limits, and I now realize teaching someone to fish is much better than giving them endless fish dinners.

Answer 44: Well, well, good job. You finally came to a conclusion. It has always been my philosophy that people have their own solution from within. They just don't trust or follow it, but the real issue is none of this would be in play if you listened to your feelings and had not softened up.

You should have stuck with your decision to break off the relationship with your boyfriend. He quit his job. You allowed him to take control of the relationship without him persuading you to keep him around. So secretly this all happened because you did not want to start dating again. You got comfortable hoping things would get better. You liked his circle of friends.

Whenever you and his friends get together, you all always had a great time. Things could have been better between you and your boyfriend if he had occasionally bought you dinner, and you were not always going into your purse to pay or slipping him money under the table. Your boyfriend needed to get his finances together. Instead of your boyfriend paying his bills (utilities, car note, and rent), he tries to buy you dinner at a plush restaurant because he thinks you deserved it, but you chose to pay. His finances would not allow him to take you away for the weekend. He does not have a girlfriend, or his lifestyle would show differently.

Now, you are growing resentment toward him for being a bystander. This relationship has started to make you feel ill just thinking about how you have supplemented his income by using yours to help him. I know you must have put on fifteen pounds of stress. When he returned from visiting with his family, he felt a sense of freedom to get back to you. He did not want his family looking over his shoulders, wondering about what he was going to do with his future since he was not working. I know he feels relieved. So you have lost your integrity by going against the grain of your feelings, by not speaking up about all your discomforts in the way the relationship had gone.

Shift tools 44: Breathe deep breaths and release any form of guilt. Create a gratitude journal and write in it nightly. Join a support group such as one of the various meetup groups.

Affirmation 44: The love I have is wonderful—wonderful when it is hand in hand, gratifying one another equally.

Issue 45: Why Won't He Marry Me?

Ms. Dorothea, hi, how are you? I have a man I love so much, and we have been together six years. Our relationship has been pretty good. No real problems. We were pretty inseparable for almost six years. He and I talked about marriage, and it is always pleasant to role-play marriage situations, but it's not cute anymore. He knows me as well as I know him. I asked him why are we not engaged. He told me it will happen just when I least expect it. Is he waiting for me to fall apart or get social security? This waiting does not make any sense. Help. I love him, but I can't stomach year seven without a ring. It's time for him to put a ring on it. Should I break up with my lover, my friend? Tia D.

Answer 45: Hi, Miss Tia. Your lover and friend is commitment-phobic. He loves you dearly and wants this foundation you guys built together to last forever, but he feels marriage changes women. He did not sign up for a bridezilla, and he never wants a divorce. You know you both witnessed this behavior from your friends. He needs reassurance that you won't change on him; this man of yours can't bear to lose you. You two need a premarital-counseling retreat so the two of you could dig deep and pull out these core fears. Then I see you will have a lush, beautiful wedding.

Shift tools 45: Premarital counseling, retreat getaway

Affirmation 45: Thank you, God, for my wonderful, loving, and caring husband. He lights up my life with joyous joy and walks in the spiritual light of heaven. I am honored for my perfect selection and give praises for the purity of our love.

Issue 46: Has My Daughter Lost Her Virginity?

Hello, Dorothea. I am wanting to take my sixteen-year-old daughter to the doctor because of all the nude picture texts she got from some boy at school, showing off his penis (a rather large one, I might add); so I've been looking to see if she has been walking funny and keeping up with her menstrual cycle. I asked her on more than one occasion if she still is a virgin, and she keeps saying yes. Help. What am I going to do? Miss Depressed and Tired.

Answer 46: Stop claiming depressed and tired. This is becoming a state of your life, and you are letting this child's immature choices drive you out of your peace. Now, you can sit down and talk to your daughter with sincerity and tell her that this behavior she is accepting from a boy is not bringing her closer to this boy. It's a topic of discussion with his boys and coaxing her to show skin as well.

Just because you haven't seen those deleted texts doesn't mean he removed them from his phone. In this day and age, because of the lecture from their parents, girls want an alternative way to have sex. It appears that a boy's penis in your mouth and pleasuring him is not sex, and I would love to say she doesn't know what the taste of a sweaty penis in her mouth tastes like, but I will be wrong. Your daughter needs to seek a competent therapist to talk to because peer pressure is real, even if it's indirect. She has placed the expectation on herself for some reason. She doesn't know how to detach from the "what other people think of me" syndrome. Many adults cannot do this either.

Shift tools 46: Books: Read these books—*Dynamic Laws of Prayer* by Catherine Ponder, *Working Inside Out: Tools for Change*, and a therapist as well to understand what teenagers are going through.

INSIGHT WITHOUT CHANGE IS MEANINGLESS

Affirmation 46: I am a loving parent. I am open to my daughter's needs, and I freely allow her to express herself.

Issue 47: Is My Daughter Dating a Boy or a Girl?

My daughter, Trina, is seventeen, and she is always on the phone with this girl, Toya. Toya comes to our home to study in her bedroom. I feel they are spending too much time together. I asked to meet Toya's parents, but I have been told that her dad doesn't live with her and her mother. I had taken Toya home and tried to meet her mother, but no luck as of yet. I asked Toya to have her mother call me.

Toya is a cute girl but has a boyish flair to her. My Trina looks like a girl and is very attractive, and she never talks about boys or going anywhere where they congregate. We go to church, but Trina hasn't brought Toya to church yet. I feel a couple of boys are interested in her, but she says that "my friend and I don't look at the boys that way." I want more variety of friends for Trina; she let all her other girlfriends from elementary and middle school fall by the wayside, and I feel Toya may be trying to seduce Trina. How can I integrate more friends into Trina's life?

Answer to 47: Trina is very attracted to Toya as if she were a boy. The two of them kissed as though they were heterosexual, but they are the same sex. In Trina's school, same-sex couples are comfortable walking the halls, mainly girls. This has been going on since she was in middle school. She is used to talking to you about anything, and you seem to be okay with it, at least that was Trina's impression. They also have experienced and explored each other's bodies, and if this is a consolation, Trina isn't pregnant.

This may be hard to hear, but Trina and Toya are a couple; and the more you object, the closer they become, and moving isn't the answer since they both are going to the same college next year. More comforting, this looks like a phase for Toya, but not Trina. I say this because I see a baby for Toya in the future, and she gets it the old-fashioned way.

Shift tools 47: Get information from PFLAG, an organization of parents and guardians of same-sex couples. This information will help you have a productive conversation.

Affirmation 47: I love my daughter unconditionally. I allow my daughter to grow and reach all her endeavors. My daughter is strong and supported.

Issue 48: Will this Man and I Have Children, Pay His Child Support and His Debts, and Live Comfortably?

Hi, Ms. Dorothea. I have been involved with my boyfriend for two years, and I want to know, Will we have kids someday? Will his ex-girlfriend stop taking him to court for more child support? LC.

Answer 48: Hello, LC, I hope you are asking me about marriage and not just having a baby with this man because having a baby with him is not the solution to keep this relationship. Despite the fact he already has children without the benefit of committing to the woman of his children, do you want this to be your fate as well? All I can say is, next!

Shift tools 48: Classes on self-esteem, along with releasing your insecurities from childhood. Let it go.

Affirmation 48: I love being with someone who values themselves and values me. I love that I attracted a healthy, loving, and committed companion that is present in my life.

INSIGHT WITHOUT CHANGE IS MEANINGLESS

Issue 49: I Want to Come Out to My Husband as a Lesbian

Ms. Dorothea, I have been living a lie for a whole year. I have been lying to my family, and now I have taken this lie into a marriage of convenience for me. My husband loves me so much, and we have dated for five years because I wouldn't marry him when I got pregnant. He and I were drinking some too-strong margaritas, and I was not taking my usual precautions, which led us to now having a three-year-old son that I adore. I am tired of living this lie and sleeping with this man; sometimes it turns my stomach to begin to have sex with him.

This is such a good guy, and he deserves someone who loves him deeply. I love him, but not the way he expects me to. I recently met someone that makes my heart jump up and down, and I cannot ever tell you when I felt like this with a man. This woman is something unique and has such a wonderful, soothing touch and a great listening ear that I just cannot stop thinking about her. The thought of her makes me get up in the morning to start my day with the anticipation of receiving a phone call from her. Even getting a picture from her by phone is exciting; my heart does flip-flops all inside my chest. Ooh, Ms. Dorothea, what am I going to do? Lost and Lesbian.

Answer 49: Hello, Lost and Lesbian. This can be very painful, being in a loveless marriage and in love with another. The bloom of love is so beautiful and exhilarating that you want to bottle it and put in your pocket, taking big whiffs of it. You are in a compromising position, which you indeed are. I know of individuals that had wonderful and horrific stories coming out to their parents, but you have to come out to yourself first, then family, your husband, and possibly your in-laws as well.

The best way to honor your desires is to trust your preferences because the only person that needs an explanation is your husband. You can take the coward's way out by getting a legal separation, asking your husband to allow you to work out some things before you ask him for a divorce. Divorce gives you an option out without exposing your secret immediately, and you may not go through a painful and embarrassing custody battle.

You are right about one thing: you have a wonderful husband that is understanding, but the issue really comes from your son. When your husband hears your confession, he has to decipher it in his head, and guess who helps him to interpret this? His mother and father. Of course, you are a deviant, and you cannot have the boy. Luckily, the courts won't see you as unable to raise a child because of your sexual preference. I don't know how much you want to be dragged through the courts.

Where you see struggle and difficulty is where you create struggle and difficulty. Where thought goes, energy flows. Energy is creative. Locate your local gay-and-lesbian headquarters and get some literature or counseling on how to talk to your husband and/or family. Listen to some of the women's coming-out stories. YouTube is an excellent source as well. Unfortunately, the baby boomers are not prevalent on YouTube, as are the Generation X and millennials. I wished wiser older individuals would take advantage of such a wonderful educational tool, but baby boomers are not about airing their dirty laundry in public, and they prefer to maintain secrecy. Imagine all the LGBTQs (gay and lesbians) of the twenties, thirties, forties, fifties, and sixties that suffered/suffering in secrecy. Some chose to die because of a life of not being able to love fully.

Shift tools 49: The first shift is for you to get in your head and stop beating yourself up. Release the curse of feeling horrible about feeling real love for the same sex and finding love for the first time in your life. To do this is by viewing and researching healthy lesbian's relationships and families. *Read*

Lesbian Couples: A Guide for Creating Healthy Relationships, *Coming Out*, and a host of other literature that is out there to give you a sense that you are not alone.

Affirmation 49: I love my skin, and I am comfortable with who I am. I love me and everything that makes up who I am. I love all my life experiences, and I love the new life I am embarking on. Love is judgeless and unconditional, and I am love.

Issue 50

My husband wants a divorce because I won't keep paying his bills and his nonworking children's bills as well. Ms. Dorothea, why should I pay my husband's bill over and over again when he doesn't appreciate me paying them off? I make well over six figures, and my husband is a project manager for a medium-sized company.

I am a contractor consultant for major corporations around the globe. I make my husband's yearly salary sometimes in two months. I love my husband and do want to help him, but I will not be anybody's fool. His children do not like me, and we are having problems putting a budget together. When we are talking, my husband resents that I bring up a budget and having his kids start living on their own.

There is so much confrontation between my husband and I. He asked me to move out for a little while so he could sort this out. I am offended, but I will move out and will be returning back home. My husband has not honored anything he said before we got married, and this is the last straw. I feel like his grown kids are more important than me. Betrayal is now the object of hurting me. He tries to obliterate any self-esteem I have; he thinks lowering my dignity will make me bend to his will. For a moment I did bend to his will. Then I got a hold of myself and walked out.

Answer 50: Unfortunately, I wish I could say that he loves you as well, but you appear to be a big, extra-fat paycheck to him. I feel you should not have disclosed your earnings so quickly to him. You mentioned to him all the things you bought for your college-educated daughter. You were lonely and thrilled when he popped the question. He does not love you, and he will start talking about divorce if it hasn't happened already.

I have a suspicion that it has already occurred because your husband wants to keep you in line, and honestly, you don't want to be alone. This man doesn't care for you, so prepare yourself. Congratulations to you for walking. By walking, it has given you a level of temporary confidence, but the divorce needs to take place. You were not valued to begin with; your marriage was filled with agendas on both parts. You no longer wanted to be alone, and he needed an extra paycheck. The grieving will not be easy. You will need a support base. Unfortunately, your family isn't much of a support, so you must find a group who values you.

Shift tools 50: Grief crying gets rid of all the built-up toxins, worrying about your marriage whether it was going to end or not. Join a "law of attraction" meet-up group in your area. Take up a new hobby, join a meetup group, or support group on how to bounce back from a divorce.

Affirmation 50: Divorce is not my status; love is my status. Love is my mantra, and I now walk in the divine flow of love, where it is always sunny and bright and full of flowing love.

INSIGHT WITHOUT CHANGE IS MEANINGLESS

Issue 51

When will my man leave his wife, and we live together? When will my man leave his wife and get a divorce? When will we live together and get married as well? CW.

Answer to 51: Ms. CW, I don't want to laugh because this is serious. I know you are serious. Your heart feels like a nervous wreck. Many men have been known to leave their spouses and marry their mistresses, being very happy. They are content and live the rest of their lives happily ever after.

In this case, it's very different because you feel like a wife to him, and you are overly needy for his attention and affection. The man you are with just wanted a woman who is sexy, serene, confident, and sassy with the great earning ability for herself so he could do as little as possible and getting as much sex as possible. He wants to have a powerful woman on his arm and an equally sexy sidepiece on the other side (if you get my meaning). Miss Lady, I see he feels you're not the one fitting this description these days.

When and if he gets a divorce, he will leave you as well because your job was to get him through his marriage. When he becomes a free man, he can do what he wants, roaming, being a free, single man, no longer lying to women to get what he wants. Sorry, your time and efforts are being wasted.

Shift tools 51: You need to read *The Heart of the Soul: Emotional Awareness* by Gary Zukav. Watch Oprah's Sunday Soul Sessions on Own to start building a better awareness. Stretch your body twenty minutes a day in the evening.

Affirmation 51: This world houses billions of people, and I am attracting an emotionally, physically, mentally, and a presently available companion. We meet one another needs easily, effortlessly, and perfectly.

Issue 52: Is It Wrong to Stay with a Man Who Has Cheated on Me?

Is it wrong to stay with a man who has cheated on me for the last eighteen years? We have a son that is eighteen years old, which is how long he has cheated on me. He has cheated with me on his baby's mother up until their kids turned eighteen and twenty-one. Then he completely dumped her by stopping payment for her mortgage, utilities, car insurance, and taking care of their disrespectful children. His daughter got pregnant and did not finish college, who claims she has daddy issues. She uses that as an excuse for her being disrespectful to my son, which is her stepbrother. This is the man I want to marry, needless to say; he has been paying my rent for the majority of eighteen years, and I am a little nervous given his track record with his baby mommas' that he has abandoned physically and financially.

When our son goes to college, he is supposed to take care of his financial needs and take our relationship to the next level. Recently I found out that he has been staying with a woman he introduced me to some years ago, and they have known each other since high school. Also, they've bought investment homes together and live in a mini-mansion together. I can't let go of the hope that he will leave all of them alone and settle down with me.

Answer 52: Hope usually gives us a feeling of inspiration to continue on a specific journey. I see hope has kept you in a holding pattern. While watching all his comings and goings, you were not getting any closer to this man of steel. He has been able to move women in and out of his life like dandelions blowing in the wind. He has been with many women since the two of you never really lived together.

The woman he met at his high-school-reunion committee has seen more of him than you have. The original set of kids he has, their mother seemed to have gotten a lot more than you have in the deal. It appears they had more of a marital arrangement because he has financially taken care of her and her household needs. Her dependency and cheating on him with a good friend of his was the catalyst for breaking it off and putting her out of the family home, which she raised the kids in.

Your son will be leaving for college at the end of this year, and once he has gone, his father will be corresponding more with him than you and giving him money directly as well. Your son's father has hope that he will run his company. He wants him to come into the business with him, which doesn't leave a lot of room for you. The better part of eighteen years your rent has been paid, you should have at least $30,000 in the bank, if not $60,000 as a cushion for all the years of uncertainty.

Your job gives you something that his first set of kid's mother did not have—a form of independence. That's why he never asked you to leave your job because the odds are, you can take care of yourself when that boy leaves your home. I know he has made promises of buying you a home; you know as well as I that promises are made to be broken. Your son's father doesn't like to improve the status of a woman unless she has the resources to do it for herself (I know this sounds ridiculous, but he is ridiculous). Then it is a competition for him to elevate her status to the levels she has not thought about becoming.

You are with a man that takes lots of pride of being way above the women in his life, and the only successful woman he has ever been with is his high school love because she knew him well. She also has a big-time corporate job with perks that can help elevate his status. It's time to prepare yourself to be able to pay all your bills solo because once this boy is out of your home, there really isn't any reason for his father to stay in touch with you unless for nostalgia's sake.

Shift tools 52: Enlist a life coach to help shift from dependence to independence. Mirror work is needed; deep belly breathing is needed as well. Grieving and tears are coming, but don't look at this as depressing. Look at it as a cleansing.

Affirmation 52: I am worthy of love and the power of being clear on what I deserve, and I bring into reality perfect wealthy, giving, gentle, loving, attractive husband.

Issue 53: I Am Having a Hard Time Trusting My Boyfriend.

Hi, Ms. Dorothea. I am asking for some insight into my relationship with my boyfriend. I cannot talk to him because I do not trust him. He wants me to talk to him about my problems and frustrations. I can talk to everyone else in the world, but not him. I caught him texting his ex-girlfriend; it appears she was doing all the texting, but he ignored her texts. All of a sudden, he started returning the texts when we, of course, split up for about a month. I told him, "If you want to be with her, then you should be with her, and you can get out." We got back together a month later, but I still do not trust him. I cannot get past the feeling that he is using me to get on his feet and then he'll leave.

Answer 53: There is a sabotage in place. You have welcomed your boyfriend back into your life and placing undue emotional restraints on the relationship since you chose not to trust him. So which is it, working on the relationship, or sending him packing? This is no abracadabra; this takes work. You have committed to "work" by bringing him back into your life.

Shift tools 53: I will purchase the secret to long-lasting love book called *The Five Love Languages* by Gary Chapman.

Affirmation 53: I choose to think positively about my relationship. I am loving and deserve love. Therefore, I am receiving love every day.

Issue 54: I Am Tired of Losers

Hi, Ms. Dorothea. I love romance and breathe it. So when I meet men, and we start going out, I like to enjoy my company, suggesting a picnic in the park. I always add my little touches of wine in the picnic baskets with some other goodies, flowers, and delicious things to eat. My baskets of assortments are a signature part of my personality. Well, it's the hopeless romantic in me; even when I am alone, I do romantic touches for myself. For instance, I love to eat next to my fireplace with lit candles (depending on what time of year), and I like to walk in the park whether by myself or with someone else. However, surprisingly, I am tired of being the one to plan everything. Even my family and friends tell me what they want me to do. I'm tired.

Answer 54: So let's start with "I'm tired." That's not a good affirmation. You are stating you are a tired individual, which gives you the character of being tired. Let's affirm your new loves are just as romantic as you, and you no longer do all the planning (which you secretly enjoy doing). You are not the only person in the world that is romantic. Start dating people that are equally yoked with you instead of going out with the first person that asked you out. If you don't have anything in common, don't go out.

Shift tools 54: You should watch the movie *The Shift* by Wayne Dyer.

Affirmation 54: I am a romantic in a sea of romantic individuals, and we vibe in the sea in the same way. I love, and love loves me.

Issue 56: I Am Ready to Quit this Job and Start My Own Business

Dear, Ms. Dorothea. I want to quit my job because I am tired of making other people rich, and I am being taken for granted by my superiors. This has been going for a very long time. I am a salaried employee, and I am expected to work overtime and come in on the weekend to finish work that is never-ending.

I also found out the company has been hiring new employees and paying them more than me. These new employees are doing less work than me. This has been on my mind for quite some time. I have an idea that I think will revolutionize the yoga work or any exercise where stamina is needed with the aid of straps. Tell me if I am crazy. I need to get my courage up. Do you ever think I would own my own yoga studio? Thank you, Ms. Dorothea, for your answer, whatever it may be. C. Baker

Answer 56: C. Baker, of course, you can get your own yoga studio, but you must stop comparing yourself to everybody. This has been leading your life with despair because comparison leads to despair, and life gives you what you ask for. The salary of your colleague's salaries are salaries they negotiated and asked for. You asked for what you are receiving. Don't get mad. You asked, so now you *got it*. Check your prosperity consciousness.

Shift tools 56: Purchase these three books: *222 Prosperity Affirmation* by Justine Perry, *Open Your Mind to Prosperity* by Catherine Ponder, and *Spiritual Economics* by Eric Butterworth.

Affirmation 56: I am financially well, financially sound, and financially safe. I have all the money I need to do whatever I want, whenever I want, and however I want.

Issue 57: I Would Like to Start My Own Cake Catering Business

Dear, Ms. Dorothea. I work at a Fortune 500 company. I have a pretty good position and have a great salary, but I have a passion for baking cakes. My passion comes from being a little kid and passing the many bakeries in my community when growing up; one particular bakery called Krossmeyer gave us kids samples of their pastries. On Saturdays I used to see all the beautiful colors of cakes and pastries and smell the wonderful aroma coming from their kitchen. Lemon, strawberry, cherry, and chocolate flavoring were stuffed, tucked and swirled all over the place. Right now my tongue is salivating.

    I always wanted my own bakery, but my mother wanted a successful son, so I went to college and received my MBA, but I still have a dream and a deep desire to see people smile every day with my baked goods. Working corporate America smiles are far and few between; everybody is so on autopilot. If I am fortunate enough to retire or my company downsizes, then what? Now I am just interested in decorating and baking delicious and unusual-tasting cakes that are custom-ordered.

    I see cake competitions are big businesses and have come full circle. From when I was a kid, though, I used to watch from my bedroom window. Mr. Krossmeyer took out of his bakery some weird-looking cake designs that I would imagine now were custom orders. I must admit I was interested in competing on some of these reality shows, but I did not want any further discouragement from my wife, who is a great cook, but I bake better. I want to invest and start my cake catering business. You will never guess what my specialty is. Did you say wedding cakes? You're right. Thanks to Mr. Krossmeyer, I have a burning desire. C. Wilmont.

Answer 57: Dear C. Wilmont, you have an infernal flame of a desire going—whew—that really needs to be attended to. I feel you are compensating well by incorporating your love of baking with your corporate agenda. It works well.

Shift tools 57: You need to do fifty jumping jacks in the mirror, breathe deep, and find businesses that will place your baked goods in their restaurants and/or mail orders for you.

Affirmation 57: I rejoice in my decision with my passion for baking and putting smiles on the faces of my supporters.

Issue 58: I Got Raped by My Mother's

Husband When I Was Eighteen

Ms. Dorothea, I am twenty-eight years old, and I have a hard time going home for family gatherings and on holiday occasions. I can remember when my stepfather cornered me in the bathroom of my family home as I was getting ready to go to a basketball game with my friends. My mother was not at home. She went to spend time with her sister (my aunt) in the south who was dying of cancer.

I was in the bathroom with a towel wrapped around me and did not know my stepfather was home from work, so I had my music blasted. I was singing in the mirror, brushing my teeth, and rinsing. I saw him from the corner of my eyes and remembered what my mother had always told me—to wear my robe when I am in and out of the bathroom after my bath. I didn't listen this time because I was home alone.

Well, he saw me and was making stupid conversation and watching my every movement, especially looking at my towel, and I was feeling really uncomfortable…(tears flowing down my face). Forgive me. I had to stop. I hadn't really told anyone about what happened. Okay, I was really feeling uncomfortable, and he was looking hard at my towel. As I was trying to run in the direction of my room, he grabbed my towel. I continued to hold my towel as he pulled me toward him. I started pushing him away from me, but he held me down on the bed. I never saw him unbuckle his belt, but I saw his exposed penis (at that time I had never seen a man's penis before—it was ugly and menacing). He put his hand on my vagina and then slipped his nasty finger in me and plunged his self inside me. I screamed, crying, "Stop! Stop! Stop!" (Tears.)

This man who I called dad was grunting me and making noises; he was too heavy to move. Then he abruptly pulled out and got up. I briefly saw some liquid squirt from this penis as I ran to my room in pain and bleeding. Needless to say, I didn't go to the game. I called my stepmother to ask if I could come over to her house. I packed my bags and left my mother's house. When my mother came back from her visit with my aunt, I was not home. My mother knew this because I told her I'd rather stay with my stepmother until she came home, but I never came back home. JB.

Answer 58: Dear JB, I noticed a word you used in your letter while describing your horrific ordeal. You asked me to "forgive you." Of course, you are forgiven, but do you forgive your stepfather for assaulting you? Forgiveness is the beginning of healing; the healing does not happen overnight. You have to work this out with a competent counselor that is equipped with rape-trauma counseling. So you can begin to stop beating up on yourself. No one should experience this level of abuse. The journey of healing has its difficulties, but you must stop feeling embarrassed, afraid, and diminished.

Shift tools 58: Please read these four books: *You Can Heal Your Life* by Lousie Hays, *Dynamic Laws of Prayer* by Catherine Ponder, *Forgiveness: The Greatness Healer of All* by Gerald G. Jampolsky, and *Forgiveness with Pen and Paper* by May Liang Chiang

Affirmation 58: I am secure and safe in my world. I am protected. Thank you, Mother Father God, for never abandoning me. I am here. I am grateful, and I am healing.

Issue 59: Internet and Facebook for Social Life

Ms. Dorothea, I met a guy on Facebook that kept contacting me. He admires and likes everything on my Facebook and my group pages. So I decided to talk to him to get to know him better. We met, and I found out we had a great deal in common. He does not judge my personality and peculiarities. I really felt comfortable and excited when we exchanged telephone numbers.

In his profession, he has experienced a lot of tragedies in his life since he is a trooper. We have been talking for some time now, which is for about eleven months. I get so excited when we talk; I look forward to talking to him. I have a very stressful job and feel like he is a great reprieve when we communicate. I love to hear about how he grew up and about his family culture.

He is a different race than I am, so it so interesting to hear about his beliefs and customs that are far different than mine but intriguing and understandable. I have a lot of pictures of him, his mother's, brother, and his daughter. He is divorced, so he still is adjusting to being single, which he says he does not like. He also has moved into his own home, and his daughter occasionally visits him. He told me that he used to be an engineer, but now he is between jobs. I have helped with some of his financial needs (not wants) because his finances are sometimes tight.

I have not met him yet (he won't Skype), but we are talking about meeting each other. Recently, he sent me some new pictures of him as opposed to the young Adonis I had been envisioning. Originally, he didn't send me a picture of him, but sent me a picture of a good friend. So he sent me a picture of himself; he is a little pudgy. However, he is still intellectual, but not the complete package as some might say. I don't care at this point. He gets me.

So I went to see him at his apartment complex, and we stood outside his apartment. He did not invite me in nor did he come to my hotel room. He told me he would talk to me tomorrow. He did call me when I was driving in my rental car and when I got back to the hotel. He complained about his back and his eyes, along with some other excuse. I was pissed. Then he had the nerve to ask me for some money to fill a prescription that costs $150.00. My mouth dropped. Sincerely, Confused or Stupid.

Answer 59: Dear Confused, may I say a word to you that might help in this case: *catfish*. You did not say if you gave him any money. Are you saying you are stupid because you actually went through with meeting him? It looks like you gave him permission to take advantage of you when he clearly lied about his appearance and background. You took the desperate route to see him, knowing he lied. So do you have a bottom of pain, or are you bottomless because he felt it was okay to ask you for money? You clearly knew he deceived you, but you were okay with it.

Shift tools 59: You need to practice self-esteem excises. Go to YouTube and look at nine activities to increase self-esteem.

Affirmation 59: I am a beautiful, passionate young woman with good judgment, wonderful loves, and wonderful friendships all around that receives wonder, love, friendships from people all around.

Issue 60: Do I Blow the Whistle on Embezzling?

I work at a small plumbing company as a financial analyst, working with accounts receivable, accounts payable, and controller. I wear other hats as well. I have been doing this for five years, which I know I do an awesome task of keeping their finances in order. I debit and credit the account and do the profit-and-loss reports. I've noticed several accounts with some weird transfers. When I approached my colleague, I could not get an answer. I continued to examine my records and reports. I noticed that the money has been going to a company located out of business. What should I do? J. C. Houston.

Answer 60: Dear, J. C. Houston, the only whistle I see blowing is to the CEO of the company. I notice you and the CEO have a first-name-basis relationship. It feels like you and the CEO can have a closed-door meeting to discuss the financial discrepancy. The CEO will investigate your finds because it appears the CEO is not involved in the emblemizing. So relax. I know this is scary, but it will work out in the end. Unfortunately, not with a firing but with a demotion. Family, go figure.

Shift tools 60:

Affirmation 60: I am a powerful, confident woman that knows her job inside and out. I act when is needed and confront any challenges that arise. I am bold and fearless.

Issue 61: Will My Movie Get Into the Cannes Film Festival?

I am writing you, Ms. Dorothea, because my sister and I are film producers. I direct and produce while she is a producer that writes the screenplays. We have a small production company with a small budget. We have been trying to enter one of our films into the film festival, but it has been a struggle due to a lot of indie films.

The indie films are now a big-budget compared to our budget. Well-known actors and musicians make these films and producers that have way more access to funding than me and my sister. I feel in this industry the little guys are getting cut out of what was potentially created for the small filmmakers that didn't have a lot of money but had a good-quality film. Jae T.

Answer 62: No, I don't see your film meeting the film-festival needs. I do not even see it being viewed. You must have some important contacts like an agent or a really well-known publicist that is known for pushing their client's film. Unfortunately, this takes money. It looks like you have some names to get your film started. However, I suggest an entertainment attorney will give you some direction as well.

Shift tools 62: Release yourself from the outcome. Just breathe and see the end results.

Affirmation 62: My lifelong dream has come to fruition through diligence and doing the work I love. I only see success. Therefore, success is all there is and all I have.

Issue 63: My Mother Has Coddled

My Niece to Her Detriment

Okay, here we go. My niece (sister) has been jumping from jobs, schools, diets, men, and doctors for the past twenty years. I am at my wit's end with her because I support my mom secretly from my husband. My husband, Marvin, owns a very successful import-and-export trucking company, and The 6 Wings and Fish restaurant stands in the metro area. He wonderfully supports me very well.

Unknowingly, he supports my mother too. I am his office assistant and a lot of my money goes to helping my mother. My niece (sister) lives with my mother rent-free, which I am footing the bill, and I am tired of this. I had my niece work at one of my husband's fish-and-wing stands, and she just about ate up all the profits, feeding her friends for free while being rude to the customers.

My mother has guilt because of the rumor that my stepfather fathered my niece with my eldest sister that has passed away. I say niece or sister because we don't know for sure, and my niece looks like my stepfather, and we can't do DNA because he is no longer living as well.

Answer 63: Stop. You should have a heart-to-heart talk with your mom and come to a resolution about her expenses that have doubled. Whenever your niece comes to live with your mother or when she is in between homes, I see your other sibling has not taken on this responsibility. Why have you? Your mother has a lot of help financially and social security, along with a pension from what her husband has left to her. What is your problem?

Shift tools 63: Find the gratitude in your niece and mom and write it in a nightly journal.

INSIGHT WITHOUT CHANGE IS MEANINGLESS

Affirmation 63: I am detached and allow my niece to live her life as she pleases without judgment.

Issue 64: My Mother's Sister, Aunt Janey

I don't know how I became the caretaker and provider for my estranged aunt that did not have a relationship with my mother while she was alive. My aunt is ninety-one years old, ornery, tired, and discontent that only visited our home maybe two or three times in my life. I have lived with my parents, and I do not recollect any visits after I left home. I can remember when my aunt Janey's neighbor would call the police, the hospital, and my mom because Aunt Janey forgot what pill to take.

When this happens, Aunt Janey would call the emergency hospital for assistance then they would call to inform my mother. My aunt's neighbors would call our home after 11:00 p.m. every time she (Aunt Janey) would get into her car (wearing her nightgown and robe) to go to her doctor to check on her medicine. My aunt sleeps a lot and gets confused if it is day or night.

Sometimes at 6:00 a.m. it's still dark, and she thinks it is still nighttime, but it's early morning. When the neighbor reluctantly approaches my aunt, she gets to cursing them out. So that is when they call the police to ensure that she goes inside her house, along with calling my mother, as I said, when she was alive. My mother would call me to ride with her to check on my aunt. We would drive an hour to calm my childless aunt down. She would cause so much commotion the police would arrive and then I would have to talk to the police to let them know we would take care of her so they could leave.

My aunt does not like my mother's children because of my dad. When he was alive, she could not stand to breathe the same air as he was breathing; needless to say, she would throw some cheap shots at me (since I look the most like my dad). Both of my parents are no longer here, and my siblings…well, that is another e-mail by itself (as I breathe deep exasperatedly). I do not know what to do. L. Jenkins.

Answer 64: Dear L. Jenkins. Your only job is to do one or two things since your aunt only has you by default. She owns her own home and is feisty with just a touch of Alzheimer's. You can start looking for nursing homes or find an individual who needs a place in exchange for free rent and light caretaking duties to assist your aunt. The task is to find a reliable individual to help with your feisty aunt that will ignore her antics but at the same time is strong and gentle with her. I feel like you have been thinking about making this decision anyway.

All I ask of you is to not go on Craigslist to find the person to stay with your aunt. There are too many people on Craigslist with hidden agendas that are not in the best interest of anyone, especially not your aunt. Lately more than ever people with good intentions are steering away from Craigslist's seedy reputation and desperation (which is unfortunate; it started out as a pretty good idea). Next let's talk about your aunt's neighbor. He appears single, and I see a little spark between you two. Am I wrong or what?

Shift tools 64: Compassion-embrace exercises—learning your aunt's history, along with your family's history, which would shed some light toward compassion.

Affirmation 64: I lovingly embrace my responsibilities and always see a happy, joyous outcome for everyone's highest and best good involved.

INSIGHT WITHOUT CHANGE IS MEANINGLESS

Issue 6:

My sister slept with two of my boyfriends when I was younger, which she thinks I don't know, and now she has been flirting with my husband. Anytime we attend family functions my husband has told me he is uncomfortable being around her, and if I don't say anything to her about her behavior, he will not attend any of my family functions with me. RKJ

Answer 65: Whatever over-the-top admiration you had for your sister as a child, it should be over now, and you're a confident woman trapped in a sea of juvenile memories. Stop the madness. Do not address it at the table when you and your family are blessing the food. Take your sister aside and ask her to be on her best behavior and stop flirting with your husband and any other man there because she is disrespecting your husband, along with her own husband. Her husband is too high to care and repeatedly ignores her. It looks like her behavior has been addressed by others.

You are the person that must say something, and the other family members, including your husband, will back you up. I also see one of the younger members of your family showing your sister how she behaves on a video recorded from their phone in regards to her last episode of shameless flirting. She is waiting for someone to take the bait, but that bait is old and worn out, honey.

Shift tools 65: Look in the mirror at the grown-up version of you and see your beauty and worthiness. Look at a wonderful family you and your husband have and see gratitude for your accomplishments. Sit up straight and feel good about you. Affirm your successes and write a gratitude journal nightly.

Affirmation 65: I am wonderful and strong. I speak to anyone about what concerns me. I use my voice to voice my joy, as well as my discontent. I am received well.

Issue 66: I Cannot Seem to Get My Life Together

Dear Ms. Dorothea, I cannot seem to get on my feet. I always feel I do not have enough money to buy me anything or go on a vacation for myself. I see so many of my friends doing better than I am. They drive better vehicles, living in nicer houses, and going on vacations.

It always seems as if I don't have enough money to last until my next paycheck. I am dating, hoping to meet somebody to help me with my bills and take me places, but all I am meeting are men who need more than I do. It does not help with my rent. We cannot go to too many places because child support is eating a hole in their wallets, so I end up helping with what little I have, and I fall even more behind. This should not be my life. I am a college-educated woman, and there are people who I know have not finished college and are doing better than me. What am I doing wrong? Sincerely, Ready to Jump Off a Bridge in Despair.

Answer 66: Dear Ready to Jump Off a Bridge in Despair, your self-worth is a factor in all this. Feeling and being worthy is one of the biggest formulas you can jump into. Self-worth is the key to you having and being more. You know you are grossly underpaid, but you continue to show loyalty to the company that is doing very well financially that can afford to give you a raise.

The company you work for does not give you a raise because you haven't asked for one when your annual review comes up, and they are milking the media's melodrama about inflation, jobs moving to other countries, and downsizing America. Many people in your company are falling for it. You have a worthy skill that needs a worthy income. If you do not feel this way and start applying for jobs, your energy of low self-worth gets in the way, and you in no way can attract a decent job, especially with better wages than you already are making.

You get your résumé looked at by a professional and tweak several résumés for different job titles to apply for a job; and if a résumé doesn't really fit the job description, you're telling a recruiter or a human-resource professional that you're lazy and can't be bothered, so you will not be a good fit for a job.

Look for a new job and stop being afraid of the title because in actuality, you are doing various jobs with your company that has management titles attached to it; you're just not being paid for it. Your company hit the jackpot with you, so now it's your turn to get the return dividends on your hard work by working with a corporation that values their employees. They're few in number, but with a wonderful résumé and attitude, you'll find the perfect match.

Shift tools 66: Shift your perspective. Shift happens when you are willing to view your options.

Affirmation 66: I am happy. I boldly go in the direction of my dreams and live a life of ease and abundance. I work well with my company. I also vacation well with my friends, and I love well with my financially successful love of my life.

Issue 67: I Want to Meet My Husband

Dear Dorothea, I am a fifty-eight-year-old woman that is in great shape, and I live alone without any dependents holding me back. I own my home outright, and I have investment properties as well. When will I meet my husband? I have been alone far too long. I've been on the dating websites for far too long and haven't met anyone. I had some health setbacks that probably helped in my delay in finding a love to share the rest of my life. I have been meeting men, but they are not up to any of my standards. I do not understand why the men let their bodies go and are sickly and want someone to take care of them. I am not that woman. Signed, Lonely in the World.

Answer 67: Dear Lonely in the World, I understand you are lonely and want a healthy loving experience, but I see there are a few setbacks to this. Your health is in question. I see several surgeries with more to come. I wish you would have gone into depth with your health because I feel you will be the one who will need a caretaker, and those same men you didn't want at the time was a candidate that would've been the very ones by your side, or a nursing home. Don't judge a person by appearance. I see some warm, wonderful, loving men at your church and in your neighborhood that are interested in you. Be open to love.

Shift tools 67: Watch the movie *Heal your Life* by Louise Hay and use the tool provided.

Affirmation 67: I am open to love and my highest potential for better health, better love, and a better attitude. I am getting better and better.

Issue 68: Lies and the Other Woman

Dear Ms. Dorothea, I have been married twenty-five years, and I am so tired of my husband lying to me about how many affairs he has had in this marriage of ours. We have four wonderful daughters, and they have made us extremely proud. I have been the primary parent while my husband works over in another country (Iran or Iraq) for contract work for the better part of our marriage. He is now working locally, which means he is home a lot, and my youngest daughter gets to spend quality time with her daddy.

About three years ago, I found a picture of a little boy in my husband's old papers, and on the back it says, "Devin two years old." There is another picture that says, "Your big little man," and dated February 2001. In February 2001 my husband was overseas, and I was here in Louisiana, raising our kids. I didn't have to work because my husband provided for us very well. He was so generous; we communicated on a daily basis, so I never suspected anything.

Going through these old papers to see what to shred, I came across this photo, and I want my husband to come clean and tell me who this baby is. I put my husband's baby picture next to the boy's picture, and the little boy in the photo looks like my husband when he was that age. My husband has been denying this for three years, and I am just tired of the lies, so I am writing you. Should I pack my bags and leave him? Signed, A Betrayed Wife.

Answer 68: Dear Betrayed Wife, the answer to your question is, yes, that was his only son on that photo, and he was led to believe it as well. It was an incident of low restraint and resistance to temptation on his part. Your husband will not go into any details and will deny it because he does not have any contact with the boy. I do not see the boy. See if you can find a paper or article of a young woman hit in her car with a toddler, and they died on impact.

You may recall seeing something like that in your husband's belongings. Your husband and his overseas girlfriend will not confirm your suspicions because she and her only son are dead. Your husband is still haunted and tortured by this incident, which is why he kept renewing his contract to provide to you and the girls. He feels guilty and punishes himself for the betrayal to his family. So take comfort that your husband is made of flesh and blood, and he is not a Greek god. He is now doing the right thing for you and his family, and the two of you can have a wonderful twenty-five more years together. Forgive and release this difficulty.

Shift tools 68: Radical-forgiveness workshop with Colin Tipping.

Affirmation 68: Say your husband's name and say, "I love you. I bless you. I forgive you and release this situation to its highest and best good."

Issue 69: I Am Tired of My Hoarder Neighbors

Dear Ms. Dorothea, I am about to lose it with the people across the street from where I live. Their front yard is full of unnecessary junk that is an eyesore, and their garage is full of trash, all kinds of debris, and papers that are a fire hazard. Not only is it a fire hazard, it reduces the value of our property if we wanted to sale. I have called the City Health Department, and the neighbor, Mr. Williams, cleans just enough to be under the radar. Signed, Tired

Answer 69: Dear Tired, you are really too close to the situation that is why it cannot get resolved. Your focus is so personally invested; unbelievably, your energy is helping it stay there. Mr. Williams has neighbors that are tired as well, but they are not losing sleep like you are over this neighbor. He has a mental disorder. You claim you are a woman of God, so now you need to bless your neighbor and step into your role. The city is well aware of this and will take action when there is a time to do it; that will happen when the other neighbors release that focus. Focus on the wonderful daily inspirations that are happening in your life.

Shift tools 69: When leaving and entering your neighborhood, go a different way if you can. Focus on the beauty of your other neighbors beautifying their property. Take deep breaths, practice compassion, and send love to the unfortunate, including across the street.

Affirmation 69: I love you. I bless you. I forgive you and release you into the ether of your highest good.

Issue 70: I am Tired of Being Mr. Nice Guy

Dear Ms. Dorothea, I call myself a nice guy, and I don't bother people. I mostly keep to myself, and I don't mind helping people when I see them trying to do the right thing. I am a single guy, and I have had a couple of lady friends that I have helped by allowing them to stay with me until they got on their feet. They still have to contribute to one or two bill(s) so they can see that I am not trying to be a boyfriend, just a friend who will be there for them until they eventually get on their own feet. I had to throw one woman out because she began to get the wrong idea by answering my cell phone and complaining about why I have been coming home late or didn't come home at all.

So I finally got her out of here, and two months later she called me up, asking me how I was doing and if she could come by to see if she left anything. I told her, "*No,* you cannot come by, and *no,* you did not leave anything at my house." Every other week she calls wanting to borrow money, asking me who lives with me now, and calling to have coffee. I just filed a restraining order on her. She does not get it. Now she is calling from different telephone numbers, trying to get in touch with me. What can I do? Signed, I'm Tired.

Answer 70: Dear I'm Tired, it is the entanglement you really are tired of; this individual wanted more than just to be your temporary roommate. I see you went the traditional route with the law, and most times it works. However, when the law cannot get the individual from annoying you, then what? Well, I have a solution, and you may think it is a too-soft sell and not effective. It's time for you to infuse love in this situation and shift your annoyance to compassion. Compassion is a factor that has not entered into this equation.

Shift tools 70: Write in a daily mindfulness journal to bring you back to center. Do morning and evening guided mediations with Deepak Chopra or Panche Desai. Breathing exercises: take deep breaths twenty to sixty in and out. Take brisk morning walks.

Affirmation 70: I am safe in my world. I realize that past troublesome difficulties have no bearing on my peace and joy in my present life. I am joyous, and I attract loving quality people into my life. I am calm, healthy, strong, and powerful. Unstoppable I am. And so it is.

Issue 71: I Would Not Call Myself a Prostitute, but Men Have Been Known to Spend a Lot of Money on Me

Dear Ms. Dorothea, I love my boyfriend so much. He bought me an expensive android phone. We go on trips. We both love to ride our motorcycles; he bought mine for my birthday. He said I have been the only woman in his life that took an interest in what he likes to do. We have been looking to purchase a house together, and I will use my house as a rental property. I have so much fun with him. He enjoys being with me.

All my friends love and accept him as one of their friends. He has a good heart, a beautiful smile, and can make me holler in the bedroom, Lord have mercy. I have not accepted any calls from my old male acquaintances since I have been in this committed relationship. What would possess my boyfriend to go snooping through my belongings when he came across an old phone and charged it up to go through my text messages? I do not understand this behavior. Since he'd been snooping, he knows about the conversations on the phone with my friends and text messages. Then he repeats the text to me verbatim. Now he is not talking to me, and he took his stuff from my house and went back to his house. Help.

Answer 71: Dear Help, your wonderful love is the most untrusting guy around, and he needs to have control of most situations in this relationship the two of you have together. He cannot help it; that is his personality. I know you must have seen some signs of his controlling nature, but I would imagine that is what you liked most about him. That behavior made you feel loved and secure, you thought. He was so invested in this relationship.

It appears he wanted to marry you. Your boyfriend snooped around and found out things he did not know about you, like…he didn't really know you had rich male friends that paid you and some girlfriends for private parties to have sex, and you got paid very well extra for your friends. He heard some of the old details and, reminiscing on your expensive $750.00 android phone that he bought for you, and he downloaded Spyware. He needed more details, so he went in your previous phone you put away when you got the new phone and got an ear and eyeful. He wrote down names and numbers to get down to the bottom of your prostitution. Even though you have a day job, he still feels you are a user of men and a whore. These are the feelings he now has for you. You have to move on; even though I see him coming back, it will never be the same. He has a memory like an elephant.

Shift tools 71: Life-healing workshops such as self-esteem and empowerment. Google it.

Affirmation 71: I love and forgive myself for any pain and deceit I may have caused. I love myself, and I bless this situation and release it to its highest and best good. I am in control of my life.

Issue 72: My Lover's Wife is Threatening Me, I Got a Court Order

Dear Miss D, my name is Arell Norman, and I have been dating a married man for three years. We met on some chat line. For the first six months I didn't know he was married. This man, once he found out where I lived (because I told him), would come to my apartment, and we would get busy and hang out together. One of the friends told me that he only lives two blocks from me, so when he tells his wife he is going to the store, he usually stops by my house. We talk among other things, and once I found out he was married, I must admit I was all right with it. Then some more months went by, and I started demanding more of his time because his communication was slacking, and I would not see him for weeks at a time.

Lately I have been e-mailing him constantly. He has been ignoring me, along with my text messages. Somehow, his wife found out, and she contacted me, asking me who was I and why was I writing her husband so many e-mails. She asked, so I told her who I was and gave her some details about her husband and me. That bitch e-mailed me back some horrible things.

Once she found out I was a man, she called me everything but God. I told her it takes one to know one since we are both sleeping with the same man. Therefore, my boyfriend came by, screaming at me about talking to his wife, which I did not initiate the call; she contacted me, and I was honest.

"I love who I am, and I am not going to lie, especially when you said you wish we were married," but of course, he doesn't remember that conversation. His wife believes him, and that is fine; love really must be blind. I need to know how this court thing is going to work out.

Answer 72: You decided to stay with a married man and did not think that any pain was going to appear. Everyone involved is in some pain. It does not matter if he loved you, which he did. It does not matter about the intimate nights and days you shared with him; he loved it. It doesn't even matter if he said he loves you, which he does. He was never ever leaving his wife and children. A restraining order will be issued against you, and all your personal affairs will be exposed.

Shift tools 72: Breathe. Write forgiveness letters for sixty-five days. Write what you found grateful for this incident (when you cool down).

Affirmation 72: I date available, loving males that are single, who love and appreciate me for who I am. I love and appreciate me for who I am. I forgive myself for any pain I may have caused and bless this situation and release it to love.

Issue 73: I Had No Luck in Finding a Man at Church, Should I Go to Home Depot?

I want to find a whole man, where we can grow with each other, trust one another, learn to be friends as well as lovers. Eventually we can look at our plans to be together for the rest of our lives, that too hard? Signed, Am I Wanting Too Much?

Answer 73: No, you are not wanting too much, but your expectations are too out of the ballpark for you because of the life you created for yourself. You want more from a man than you are willing to give because you met some wonderful guys over the years.

Unfortunately, we live in economically tight circumstances for some. Although I see men wanting exactly what you want, the ones you have met and got to know cannot pay all your expenses to give you the life of luxury. Like a wise woman once told me, if you want to date millionaires, then you have to associate with millionaires, Not men whose ex-wives are taking them to court for increases every six months.

Shift tools 73: What are you bringing into the relationship that is attractive for a man to say you are the one? Edit your list with this in mind.

Affirmation 73: I have a healthy outlook on my right and perfect relationships, and I bless my life with love and mutual sharing with my husband.

Issue 74

Hi, Ms. Dorothea. I have a question for you and thank you in advance for answering it. Will my dad put in his last will and testament that I have controlling factors over his land and properties? Due to my parents being up in age. If my dad passes away before my mother, I'm afraid of how my mother will handle everything since she doesn't listen to anyone, and she can be promiscuous. A man could come into my mother's life after my dad passes away and marry my mom (my mom never loved my dad, in my opinion), and this new man in her life could very well inherit the family heir's property. Can I convince my dad to put it in my name or make me executor of his will? What can I do?

Answer: 74: Your dad does not trust you or your brothers; that is why you did not mention you had other siblings. For your father to place you in the seat of power over his affairs, he will instantaneously assume you are trying to bump him off. Release your anxiety. It is high when it comes to you and your siblings.

I see one brother bullied you at times, and you really feel that your brother is trying to get the upper hand with your father to take away your piece of the pie. Everything moves smoothly when you release your anxiety over this matter; and for your mother, she's displaying early Alzheimer's behavior. You need to come to grips why you feel you cannot trust your brothers. I know one was particularly rough with you when you were youngsters. You must heal from all that roughhousing and see yourself as a capable adult, just as your father sees you.

Shift tools 74: Stretch your torso, and find a yoga practice that fits your need. Get a forgiveness counselor or therapist to talk to, to help you release sibling anxiety.

Affirmation 74: I seek and see only good, fair, and honorable outcomes. I let go of all that's not for my highest and best good.

Issue 75: Will My Health Improve?

Ms. Dorothea, will my health improve? I am an avid healthy eater, and I give a lot of attention to my health because my family does not have good health or have good health practices. When an illness arises in my family, that is when they want to flood the hospitals with why they're having the health difficulties they are having and want to sue the doctors for the destruction of their health. They want the doctors to be miracle workers with their severely unhealthy lifestyle and practices. I do not get it.

My family does not want to take responsibility for their behavior, but I have to take responsibility for my behavior. I am juicing daily, detoxing, taking vitamin supplements of iron, zinc, vitamin C, turmeric, cinnamon, B-complex supplements, kelp, bromelain, ginger, ginkgo biloba, magnesium, selenium, along with hair and nail vitamins due to my thinning hair. I take food grade hydrogen peroxide once a day. I do kettle ball three times a week along with my trainer. I bike four times a week. I only eat fish and organic fruits vegetables. I want to get away from my family's health history, and I don't have any of the so-called hereditary illnesses my family has. I am fifty-eight years of age, and I still sometimes fluctuate from 115 to 125 pounds. I want to know why.

Answer 75: I applaud you in your taking a wonderful interest in your health, and from what I can see, this is working for you. Hormonally you are losing a great deal of estrogen, and you may need to look into this more with the health provider or alternative health provider of your choice. There are wonderful all-natural creams that can provide what your body needs, such as a cream called A Woman's Touch, but I strongly suggest you check this out with a health professional before incorporating this in your routine.

Shift tools 75: Release the anxiety of aging. Look to wonderful people who are aging or ageless and are having a healthy balance of work, play, and exercise in their lives. Cher's mother gave a wonderful quote for her girls: "Don't worry about age, and age won't worry about you."

Affirmation 75: I love my age, and I am ageless. Life is filled with wonder, and I am in its playground of pure possibility.

Issue 76: A Great Introduction

Ms. Dorothea, I was introduced to a guy named Phil through my colleague. We have been dating four or five months. Now he acts enamored by me; he can't keep his eyes off me when we're together. Since I just started sleeping with him about three weeks ago, he can't keep his hands off me whether he is caressing my skin, holding me, hugging for long periods at a time. I am pleased with him.

Phil recently came clean and told me he has never been faithful to any woman, but since I came into his life all bets are off, and he wants an exclusive relationship with me. He talks about moving in together and possibly getting married. I must admit, all this takes me back, and I don't know what to think about all this. I am not ready to trade in my independence to be his live-in girlfriend. I have not seen any house cleaners, cooks, dishwashers, and/or laundry attendant at his place, so who is supposed to do that? Not me. I really do care about him and feel like the only woman in the world when we are together, but there may be a red flag or two. What should I do? Nobody's perfect.

Answer 76: Well, hello, Miss Lady. You are right in your assessment—he is quite taken with you, especially when you do not complain. He feels as he is doing everything right in your eyes. At least you appear to be pleased with all he does. I have a question for you: Why did you say you were sleeping with him for only a few weeks? In my assessment, you guys look like you were sleeping with each other after one week of knowing one another.

Now let's get back to basics. Phil came clean because he needed to get that out of the way. He was telling the truth when he said he has never been faithful to anyone else, and he is not going to start now. He dates the women of many races and loves the variety. He wants to be known as an international lover, especially with women of color. This boyfriend of yours takes a lot of pictures, I would imagine, to brag to his brother and colleagues. It almost appears he has a harem stable of pretty women with different ethnic backgrounds.

As a Caucasian man, he loves the variety, and it feels like he is dating and sleeping with all those beautiful women on

TV; but don't get me wrong, he is an executive with his company. His company has recently experienced some financial difficulties. That is why he is renting an apartment. Your decision about him has some selfish reasoning as well. I see you are enamored by him as well, and he is the best lover you had up to date.

None of your previous men you had been dating had the skill of Phil. He explored your body as though he was mining for gold and hit the jackpot several times in a row. Something tells me you know this, and it gives you pleasure throughout the day, thinking about what he did the night before.

Don't worry. He has no intentions of the two of you moving in together because to see him two nights a week doesn't appear to me like his old habit has gone away at all. Phil works from home and does not have to leave town for business. He is in town, dating someone else. It's an app that says he is calling you from a different city. He is seeing some of the same women for years. You are just the new kid on the block.

Shift tools 76: Break up. Breathe. Take many cleansing, deep, deep breaths throughout the day. Listen to your favorite uplifting music, really uplifting. Do not go to those sad, lonely victim songs. Exercise outdoors and join a boot camp to help release the anger and to start your day off right. Write in a gratitude journal. Read *The Twelve Steps to Forgiveness* by Paul Ferrini. Be willing to forgive.

Affirmation 76: I love that I attract whole, healthy, monogamous men into my life. I am loving and worth loving, and I have monogamous relationships.

Issue 77: Why Did I Lose All My Properties?

I lost all of my properties in the nineties, and I still haven't really recovered from that.

Answer 77: You are supposed to be in prison due to how you fraudulently acquired all those properties. Losing those properties was a gift and a slap on the wrist from the universe. You lost all your properties due to poor money-management skills. You haven't, at the time, conquered balancing your checkbook, and now you are a big-time property tycoon. Well, not a tycoon, but for as many as you had, it felt like you were a tycoon.

The reason you are not behind bars is your loving nature and not wanting to hurt people in spite of your goals. You were fair and caring since you kept your word to the people you dealt with. However, you dealt with shady business people you decided to trust, so the business relationships and your property fortune went down the tubes due to a contrast in energy. You wanted properties through any means necessary because you saw that as a way to financial freedom. Money management was never your forte, and judgment of character has always been your biggest downfall. Your saving grace is your love and respect for people. You always kept your word to them no matter what.

Shift tools 77: Your true path in life is your destiny. The gift you run away from that was supporting well.

Affirmation 77: I am good to God's children on planet earth, and I am good to myself. I bless and forgive any and every one I hurt unknowingly and those who have hurt me. I walk in light and love.

Issue 78: Why Won't This Woman Take This Money?

I keep calling this woman who has decorated my home, and she won't return my calls to take the last payment I owe her for finally completing the visionary task in my home. It finally has the look and feel of what I wanted. She is not answering my text, e-mails, and phone calls.

Answer 78: Let me be clear. You are asking me why this woman, who sounds like your interior decorator whom you been having an affair with, whom you insulted her style and her expertise, won't return your calls. Not only that, you accused her of not doing all she promised with the down payment you paid her and the other subsequent monies given to her to create your vision. Your overbearing personality was eventually too much, and the affair did not have a lasting value for her to even see you again.

So you want to know why she doesn't take the last payment? She doesn't want it. Haven't you been praying to get ahold of your financial responsibilities? Well, here is a little extra to add to it. Someone anonymously told the interior decorator's husband about her affair the two of you were having, and they are in counseling with really no hope for saving her marriage, the marriage she loves. Do you know anything about this? I think you do, and so does she. That is why she is not answering. Any other questions?

Shift tools 78: Check out your behavior of how you treat people who are in service to you. Let go of the "king of the world" attitude and develop compassion.

Affirmation 78: I have compassion for all the service personnel in the world and behave lovingly and respectful of their craft.

INSIGHT WITHOUT CHANGE IS MEANINGLESS

Issue 79: Will I Get My Dream Home,

A Frank Lloyd Wright?

Dear Ms. Dorothea, I have been wanting a Frank Lloyd Wright home for as long as I can remember. My wife and I have taken tours throughout the country where his homes are developed. I really would like to own a Frank Lloyd Wright. Since my wife and I are retired, we are ready to start living our life. I am now on a fixed income, and I have to be careful with our money, but I want this dream to come true. Will it?

Answer 79: Hello, Frank Lloyd Wright enthusiast. Yes, you will get a home of your dreams. It may not be in the state you want it to be due to your wife's climate sensitivity. I know you do not want to make her unhappy. Your dream of getting a Wright home is in a warm climate, but it looks like your home won't be. You will acquire a Wright home when you least expect it.

Shift tools 79: Relax and release the anxiety attached to your search release and know you will receive. You have done the groundwork let it come.

Affirmation 79: I trust and believe that divine power helps and heals. Thank you, kind spirit.

Issue 80: I Am Ready to Elevate My Career in Media

Hey, Dorothea. What do you think about me getting a better career in media? I have worked in the media field for about thirty-five years and in many different states. Now I'm on the local scene, and I had some bites in the recording sector, pulling in a large audience. I do have some fears that in this youth-oriented culture, an old bird like me will be phased out soon, but locally, I'm doing exceptionally well. When will I leave my pond in favor of the ocean?

Answer 80: Dear Ocean lover, you are exceptional and dynamic. Youth or no youth, that personality of yours is priceless, even more so effortless and natural. I understand your fears and why youth is so attractive, but I see you understanding your audience as well with your wandering eyes. You don't practice what you want—youth and young women. This is what you have on the brain every time an attractive young woman catches your eye. It doesn't mean you have to catch her phone number as well.

Your actions should not be on these attractive women. These women are physically fit, mature women with savvy and grace whose outgoing, risqué behavior you're in favor of. Practice admiring beautiful women of all ages, and this would be more effective if you were a bachelor. Your behavior could make one quick-witted fool even though she has successfully pulled the wool over your eyes. Your wife is one of those classic, beautiful, ageless, physically fit women (ask her young lover who wants her to leave you).

Alimony is nobody's friend, and she would get it. In addition, karma really is the bitch of betrayal; it keeps you from having your dreams realized, which is right in front of you. I feel you still love that small pond and do not want to share it with sharks who will do anything to get to the top. Are you ready to go and get into the frigid water to play with the pseudo Ivy Leaguers of the broadcast world?

Shift tools 80: Count your blessings, see gratitude, and honor the people who put the work into making you look good. Sing their praises and honor that classic beauty you lay with every night.

Affirmation 79: I am successful and well recognized for my pioneering talents and tenacity that keeps me well balanced and popular for years to come.

Issue 81: A Digital Recorder Did the Deed

Dear Ms. Dorothea, you confirmed the suspicions I had in our last session without me telling you directly about what was going on. I truly found out that my wife does not want me anymore and has had multiple affairs in our home while I went to work and traveled for work. I have invested in several digital recorders and placed them around the home. I secured them tightly in places where they would not be exposed, and I got my answers.

I wrote down where I hid them in our home so I wouldn't forget where I placed the recorder. In her vehicle, I found four of the recorders, but I can't find the fifth one. My wife does not appear to have found the recorder, but if she did, all I can say is, she is a damn good actress and missed her calling. Did my wife find the fifth recording device?

Answer 81: No, Ralphy or Rascal or whatever the dog's name is found it. The dog buried it near some shrubbery and portions of the recorder are in broken pieces all outside your home. This was some time ago. I think it is safe to say your wife did not find this recorder. What is the incentive to keep finding evidence of your wife's infidelity and still nothing is done? You keep being tortured, and you have the ability to not torture yourself.

Shift tools 81: Release your torture and take some action. Either way, talk to a professional to give you your choices. Healing has to take place no matter whatever your choice is, and it begins with you. What does a healthy relationship look like, and where have you seen and known examples of that?

Affirmation 81: I take action in whatever I do. I love and respect myself first, and I get that same love in return.

Issue 82: I Am Seventy-Two and Still Got It Going On

I am an attractive, single seventy-two-year-old female, and I was recently asked by a twenty-two-year-old young man if I would be his woman. He said it took a year to get the nerve to talk to me, and we are having casual conversations whenever I run into him. This young man asked me where my man was.

I told him, "Working. He travels."

He said, "Get rid of your man and allow me to be more attentive to your needs."

Whenever I see this young man, he can't take his eyes off my large, voluptuous, curvy hips and butt. I asked him how old he thought I was, and he said forty, no more than forty-five years old.

Answer 82: You are absolutely right. He cannot take his eyes off all that junk in the trunk, as he calls it. This man can't stop talking about you to his coworkers whenever he sees you, so he is sincere. One of the biggest attractions is your curvy, shapely hips that fascinates him, and he only knows you are an older woman. He has no earthly idea your age since you don't look it at all. An older woman, in his opinion, can handle his massive penis and have enough experience to give him pleasure as well as he gives you pleasure.

The young girls his age cannot handle his size and do not enjoy having sex with him. He is very successful with older women that have childbearing hips. Your sexy sassiness has added extra attention to him; he just got to have you. To get rid of him, talk to him about spiritual matters and armed forces. When he asks for a ride home, it's because he wants you to know where he lives so you can come over all the time.

Make him pay for you to take him home to show him you are not flattered by his penis size.

Shift tools 82: You know you are a vibrant, sexy woman, and age is nothing but a number.

Affirmation 82: I love my age. Thank you, kind spirit.

Issue 83: Housing Units Going Bust

I have several housing units, and I want a smaller rate, so I am refinancing the properties. I was told to put money in an escrow account and to stop paying the mortgage company. I was told the refinanced agency will pay and give me a better rate. Well, I'm getting notices of foreclosure, and it is frightening. The refinance company is giving me the runaround and not making any sense. What is going on?

Answer 83: You're being ripped off by this pseudo refinancing company who isn't paying any of the mortgages. They are embezzling the money you put up in good faith. This refinancing company does not have a good rating with the BBB and is being investigated. Your properties are not going to be refinanced by them. Go back to the original loan holder, be honest, and show them what has been done to obtain the lower interest rate. Then I see your properties will be taken out of foreclosure, and the loan holder will refinance you. You may not get the lowest rate, but at least it is legitimate and safe. Your properties will be safe.

Shift tools 83: Release panic. Help is on the way. Honesty is the best policy. Take action by finding a more-creditable law firm or mortgage company for refinancing your home.

Affirmation 83: I handle my responsibilities with effortless ease. I give thanks for the remarkable life of possibilities and for the action I take daily to bring into successful reality.

Issue 84: My Cousin and the Wrong Decision

My aunt is in her early to middle nineties, and she recently stopped driving. I have been helping her with her errands, doctor appointments, and banking from time to time. I bring food to her from a local food bank that overfills boxes with an abundant array of her favorites. I receive the food, but I do not cook her meals. My aunt still cooks, so when I am over her house, I do not let it go to waste, and she appreciates the fact I do eat her food. I notice how she handles her money. Every time she goes to the grocery store, she has $1,000 cash money to buy groceries. I tell her she does not need to take $1,000 every time she grocery shops. She pulls the money out in front of everybody.

One time she pulled out her money, I could not get to my vehicle fast enough out of fear, hoping nobody would hit us over the head to rob us. I had to sit for a while to release the fear once I got her in the car on the passenger side and locked the doors. I had to take deep breaths to compose myself. My next visit with my aunt was that she needed to go to the doctor.

After her doctor's visit, she went to the window to pay her bill and pulled out another $1,000 to pay the doctor. She already has her medical visits paid for. I told her to put that money away. We went to the bank, and my aunt was talking to the bank teller. She got confused on what the bank teller was asking. I tried to decipher what my aunt wanted, and we got it done eventually.

This was nerve-racking. I can't do this anymore, so I have made the decision to call her son (my cousin) in Atlanta. He needs to come to help his mother (my aunt) with her affairs. I was a little reluctant because he owes me $500.00 and has never paid it back. I explained to him about his mother's situation, and he came down to have a talk with her, but he does not visit her that often. My aunt is very independent, and she doesn't care for his wife and kids.

Two weeks later my aunt called me late one evening frantically to say somebody is stealing her money out of her account. She put me on two-way as she called the bank. The bank asked her for her code, which she did provide, and the automated voice told her of transactions she had not done.

We called customer service since it had twenty-four-hour customer service helpline, and to no surprise, her son, who she allowed to obtain power of attorney over her affairs, was paying his bills and spending her money like he just won the sweepstakes. Customer service said there was no tampering with her account.

Then my aunt said to me, "He's spending my money like I was already dead in the ground."

So I said, "Let's tell Momma [my aunts' sister] your son is ripping you off."

Then she got indignant and embarrassed, saying, "That is my son. He is spending what is his by right anyway. If he wants to spend it, then it is his right and nobody else's business. If my son wants to chop off my head, he can do so, and it is nobody's business."

What have I done?

Answer 84: Well, to your surprise, you put your aunt's affairs in the hands of a compulsive spender and gambler. Your cousin's wife does not know he has his mother's money and spending it like water while paying off his small loans he has taken out over the years. He has not ever paid his mother back for the loan she lent him to purchase his house that his wife knows nothing about. Your aunt is petrified and cannot sleep because she keeps looking at the money leaving her account, and she is helpless to do anything. She feels she will soon be out on the street since she bought another home and has a mortgage in her nineties.

Shift tools 84: Prayer line and prayer partner. Call prayer line.

Affirmation 84: I am not disturbed by my honest intentions. I choose peace above all else and am willing to see the blessings in love and intention.

Issue 85: I Am So Ready to Retire

I am wondering, if I sell my business and call it an early retirement, where do you see me afterward?

Answer 85: In Florida buying a beautiful property near the beach and being in love with your new beau and finding even more love, which you will have to choose. You love your life, and you start another small business, which is super successful. You have the Midas touch.

Shift tools 85: The journey is waiting for you. Go confidently in the direction of your dreams

Affirmation 85: I deserve and have the life of my dreams. I am finally living God's dream for me.

Issue 86: Why Is My Mother Such a Bitch?

My mother has never really loved me, and I felt this my whole life. Now that I am a mom, I have had a setback in my marriage and career choices. I have confided in my mom, who you would think would want to help me or at least give me some great advice. No, she calls child-protection agency on me to have my kids taken away from me, and I had to fight like hell to keep this from happening, and I know it was my mother. I don't talk to anyone else.

Answer 86: Well, you did not need me for the answer because you are right. What you do not know is, this is your third lifetime with this woman, and in the last two lifetimes, you were horrible to this woman. You had her children taken away through wealthy family members, which is why she cannot stand or tolerate the rich in this life. In this life, the table was turned. She is in the seat of power over you because if you can stop looking for approval, she can finally love you. Give it up.

Shift tools 86: Practice and learn compassion for her pain. Forgive your mother for your pain.

Affirmation 86: I bless and love my mother. I forgive her and release her so I may go free to live and happy and fulfilled life.

Issue 87: Will We Adopt?

My partner and I have been trying to adopt. We have been running into brick walls and discouragement. Will it ever happen?

Answer 87: No. I do see you having your own baby. You ask me how can two men have children. Well, I see two children that look like each other. It looks like there is a big business to have foreign women, for instance, in India to be implanted with your sperm and carry your baby to term. It is called assisted reproductive technology. Surrogacy is the answer, and it's legal and legitimate, and the best part of it all—the babies will have your DNA.

Shift tools 87: Do your research. Relax.

Affirmation 87: I am a happy father and love seeing the smiles on my children's faces daily.

Issue 88: My Friends Mean More to Me Than My Family

Hi Ms. Dorothea, I have been having a problem with my stuck-up family. They look their noses down on people who do not live as well as us. I must admit we live very well; my parents have a prominent career, and I don't want for anything at all. I guess that's because I am an only child and have been a straight-A student since elementary school. My parents are putting a lot of stock in me for the future. They want the best for me, and I understand that. They don't understand me and won't give me back my car keys. I am not failing one grade in school. I was told by my parents they received a call that I was not in class, so my punishment was to take my car keys away from me for a class I don't need.

This is my senior year of school. C'mon. I am staying with my boyfriend. I love to visit my boyfriend and his family. It feels like a new world for me. The neighborhood is filled with people smiling, fussing, dancing, and music always playing. When I enter the front door of my boyfriend's house, I am greeted by food being cooked by his mom. You can smell the fried chicken, mashed potatoes, fried porkchops with onions, corn on the cob, string beans, corn bread, rolls, macaroni and cheese, and Jell-O for dessert. I can hear the table being set as I sit on my boyfriend's bed in his bedroom. His sister is complaining as usual that nobody is helping her set the table for dinner.

My boyfriend is in his room, counting money in front of me because he trusts me, and I always have my own money. The money he is counting is from his drug business, which he is hiding from his siblings and me. He tells me to get washed up for dinner as he hides his money in his room under the vent in his ceiling. My play mother-in-law always asks me to stay for dinner. She is a great cook and is always cooking too

INSIGHT WITHOUT CHANGE IS MEANINGLESS

much food for her greedy children. My mother never cooks unless it is in the form of takeout.

Mr. Charley, my boyfriend's stepdad, is always on time for dinner after playing dominoes with his friends outside most of the day. Then my play mom begins fussing about washing up, and everybody sits down to eat. I am here because I love the people, music, people cooking food in their homes, cooking on big black barrel trash containers turned into grills, corner restaurants, and stores with bulletproof glass in the businesses, buses, and trains going by, along with the police going up and down neighborhoods as well. It is all exciting: people hustling furniture, footwear, clothes, toys for kids, fruits and vegetables. Music and card-playing old men in the parks and young men playing dominoes on the corners. I love the feel of life here, the interaction of people doing the everyday survival.

My mother and father do not understand why I spend so much time down here, and I tried to explain it, but of course, they don't hear me. My dad used to live in environments like this growing up, and now he acts as if he is better. I want my car keys; it does not matter with or without a car. This is where you could usually find me.

Answer 88: Your grandfather was exceptionally smart, and his children got some of it, but you got most of his brainpower; it skipped his children, and his granddaughter got his intellect. You got it all, in my opinion. You feel like a genius and can accomplish any goals you set for yourself when you go to college. That's how brilliant you are. You are being taken for granted of how well you absorb the math and sciences; you eat it up and take no prisoners. What a powerful gift for a young woman like yourself to have and accomplish.

Your parents have put you in an area where there is no drive-by shootings or young girls being kidnapped and put into a life prostitution or worse. Sometimes you come home, and you are not greeted by anybody, no dinner being cooked, no aroma coming out of the kitchen, Mom still working, Dad upstairs catching up on all his shows for the week on the DVR. To you, the house always feels lonely and empty, and on top of it, you are an only child. Do you really think that if people had your choices, they would stay in a low-income environment or choose yours? Of course, it would be yours. Inner city can be fun, but it is hard living and surviving as well. Mothers are mostly the same. They want their children to have all the opportunities that life has to offer—plain and simple.

You have a fetish or a longing for life in the inner city because it feels like you're missing something. I see your love for your boyfriend's family and your love for his mother. She is easy to talk to more than your parents. Your long talks are nice, but she has told you she feels there is something so much better for you elsewhere. She lives in a place where people feel trapped in their lives and stuck by their circumstances.

You (little girl) play at being inner-city hard, and your friends love you genuinely and are a little jealous as well. You live in a better neighborhood with two parents and do not have to share anything due to being an only child, a brat they feel you are, but love you still. Your boyfriend has prosperity consciousness and makes lots of money illegally, but he has an innate criminal-and-crime lifestyle that goes much further than his environment. Him being so young maneuvers people and can make money better than some CEO of large companies. He has an inner timing of things that he cannot explain, and a few people are paranoid, who thinks he's a snitch or a cop.

The guys around him can't explain his Teflon reputation; that is because your boyfriend was a 1930s gangster in his former life. He brought back this instinct of underground whiskey and liquor trade during Prohibition from his past life (which he doesn't know anything about in this life). He plans

INSIGHT WITHOUT CHANGE IS MEANINGLESS

to leave the inner-city life in favor of a life like your parents. That's why he likes you. I believe he will amass a fortune peddling what he peddles, and you picked him out of all the boys around to fall in love with.

I see you will always attract wealth, but this life is exciting with your friends and boyfriend. You love inner-city life, and it is hard to believe from your friend's perspective you love where they live better than your vanilla neighborhood of boring house and empty streets, as you so eloquently put it on many occasions. I must tell you, your boyfriend will not live to be a man of old age. For the most part, there is a countdown clock with his name on it. When you go home, you do not see people. You see garage doors opening and cars driving out and garage doors closing while cars drive in. You hear birds in the day and crickets at night in between its quiet.

Your friends have fun all the time and live for the moment, not thinking about the future, who has more to lose. Look around, especially when you are in the car with your boyfriend and his friends. Who in the car has something to lose? Think about it. keep it up, Miss Lady, and you are going to be the only dumb genius behind bars with no probation, and you will not be eligible for parole for at least ten years all because of your choices and the company you like to keep. Keep it up.

Shift tools 88: Appreciate your life and your surroundings. Stop taking your life for granted and all that your parents worked for. See deep into what you really have. Start a gratitude journal involving your parents and all they've sacrificed for you to keep you from being a statistic in an environment where you could get lost.

Affirmation 88: There go I if not for the grace of God

Issue 89: Issues, Issues, Issues, I Got Issues

Dear Miss Dorothy, when will my man come back home? He left Friday two weekends ago.

Answer 89: Your boyfriend is like a cat, who likes free food and a comfortable bed with a woman who won't complain much, and if you do complain, it won't do you any good. Give him a few weeks; he will be back. Cats will always find their way back to food that's easily provided.

Shift tools 89: Visualize your dream man who does not stray and enjoys spending time with you. Do this five times a day in front of a mirror. Do not be alarmed if a different face shows up other than your present man.

Affirmation 89: My heart welcomes my permanent love. I am alive with appreciation and love for this permanent relationship.

Issue 90: Ejaculation Problems, or Is It?

Hi, Ms. Dorothea. I have been with this guy of mine for three years, and he has grown children with an ex-wife, so he really doesn't want any children. So when we make love, he can go for an hour or so, and there is never a big finish—nothing. So my bones and pelvis hurt from the force in many different directions, and uh, uh nothing.

A year ago he would ejaculate, and I was really careful to not get pregnant; but now he won't do anything, and I feel he's frustrated. He turned red when he ejaculated, and I asked him to see a doctor, which he said he would. However, he has not seen a doctor, and he does not look as though he is thinking in that direction. I want to know, what can I do to help?

Answered 90: Okay, you said ejaculation problems, which are true. He doesn't want you to know, but he has reached out from a doctor to obtain information about his problem. Delayed or acquired ejaculation is not uncommon in men his age, and you did not say, but he looks about twenty-five years older than you.

What is curious, though, is he has ejaculations when masturbating, and I know you witnessed this because he likes you to watch. He appears to be a little bored with you and has done and said some unkind things to you. You take what he says and does to you and stays. Now he looks like when you are having sex with him, you may say to him, "I know you want to choke the hell out of me." That excites him, and there you go; he is raining fluid all over and in you, but this disturbs me because when he thinks of hurting you, he cums.

So it is situational, the delayed ejaculations that happens at certain times. I see you trying to get pregnant against his will, and that's not cool because trapping him won't allow you to keep him. I know he is rich and distinguished, and you see what he does for his grown children and does not do as much for you. That is why you keep an apartment. He is ready to live, not change diapers or deal with a toddler again; so if you go through it, be prepared to have the pregnancy experience alone.

To be really honest, you had so many abortions in your life you are likely going to miscarry it anyway because any soul now doesn't want to come to the planet with a wealthy father he will never see. Not only that, an alcoholic mother as well all because you thought you could change his mind. You do not do what you want to do. Insight without change is meaningless.

Shift tools 90: Start valuing your body and stop living in fear of poverty. Date. "It's Just Lunch" is a dating company with a large database. Breathe, release anxiety and fear of being alone. A life coach is needed.

Affirmation 90: I love my own company, and I attract others that love my company.

Issue 91: When Will I Get a Boyfriend?

I'm twenty-five years of age, and I have not had a monogamous relationship yet. Oh, wait a minute, I know you must be looking at my words sideways. I mean gay relationship. I am so tired of my best friend, Natalie, dropping her plans and going with me to my family functions as my assumed (stand-in) girlfriend. No one asks if we are a couple. I feel they might hear otherwise, so we don't volunteer any info unless asked. Natalie is a doll, but she is getting tired of pretending she is my girlfriend, and I'm tired as well. When is my time coming?

Answer 91: So when are you coming out of the closet? Do you not think that is an issue in itself? Pretty much the family knows and are hoping it not to be true in every sense of the word. They like Natalie, but is she gay? Do guys alternate with each other's families or something, or are you her alibi? Really, because that is what it looks like to me, and she does not want to blow her cover; so when you eventually come out, that's seriously going to blow her cover.

You do not have any swagger, and you need to drink some muscle milk and look into weight training because you do not have any muscles. You're skinny (I am sorry to say), and you look hungry in more than one way. How are you going to be thirsty (looking for dudes) when you look hungry (malnourished)? We are not even in a third-world country. Now, c'mon. You got to get pumped and change your hair, get some spray tan or some healthy sun, ChapStick, a new wardrobe (Natalie can take you shopping for clothes to show you what her stud likes to wear). C'mon, beef it up some. They will come. Quickly.

Shift tools 91: Stop looking at what you do not want. Focus on what you do want and keep it there. Take some stock in yourself. Begin releasing fear by seeking out healthy and comfortable ways of coming out. (Really, everyone knows or have assumed you are already gay.)

Affirmation 91: I am loved and accepted by my partner's love and acceptance, and we have a healthy, wholesome, and loving relationship. I am glad he is in my life, and he's doubly glad I'm in his.

Issue 92: Yes, I'm Divorced and Bitter

Hi, Ms. Dorothea. I don't know why I'm seeking out your guidance. I am forty-one years old, divorced, bitter, alone, and an angry woman. I have been with my husband for twenty-four years, but married for twenty-one years. We have two beautiful boys almost breathtakingly handsome, and they are fifteen and eleven years old. I did everything right in my marriage. I kept my cheerleader figure, and that was not easy. I can still fit in my college cheerleader uniform and high school as well.

I supported and helped cultivate my husband's career, and he is a successful dentist with two locations. I am a pretty savvy real-estate realtor, and I'm proud to be a part of The Million Dollar Club in addition to my work. I am in a couple of philanthropic organizations to stop child abuse and childhood obesity. My husband of twenty-four years did not discuss with me that he wanted a divorce. He made the decision on his own because we never talked about divorce. He told me that he had filed for a divorce and was very generous with me and the boys.

"You pretty much get everything, and I will take care of the boy's college," he said. I told him I could read the documents myself, so he handed me the divorce papers to sign. I was stunned, paralyzed, utterly shaken to the core, and speechless, literally no words could come out my mouth. My friend, lover, confidant, and husband threw me away without me uttering a word. OMG! (tears) You cannot know what that feels like when you are in love and dedicated your whole life to a marriage and wonderful children—literally my dream since I was a little girl—without me realizing he had already packed his personal belongings and was walking out the door.

When he left, I got into bed to watch my wedding videos, child-birthing videos of my sons, and turned off the phone. For about two weeks I stayed in bed, barely eating. My poor oldest son would try to nourish and nurture me. He would prepare whatever he could find in the kitchen to feed me. Then he called my mother for assistance. I am still beside myself, asking, "What I did wrong?" I got old is the only answer I could think of. Why is this happening to me? Bitter Divorcée.

Answer 92: Dear Bitter Divorcée, tears are streaming down my face. I felt your pain, especially that baby trying to console and nurture his mother. Life can throw some devastating blows, unexpected blows that shake the very core of your being, and no one could really understand this level of pain. The twilight zone comes to mind when you give your all, and you hear the news that makes absolutely no sense. How could utter happiness fall away so instantly like a deflated balloon?

Shift tools 92: This door of rejuvenation has opened a new horizon of self-love. I recommend Reiki treatments to help you lift the pain of grief.

Affirmation 92: I am better and better every day. I am of value. I am valued. I am loved and lovable. I value myself.

INSIGHT WITHOUT CHANGE IS MEANINGLESS

Issue 93: What Is He Doing, Dorothea?

Dorothea, I have been with this man for over twenty years, and we have been married for fifteen years. I cooked, cleaned, worked, and provided him with a home he could be proud of. I have kept myself looking good for him and did not have a whole lot of girlfriends in out of our house nor on the phone.

Several years ago he did not work due to his back problems. Now we got that under control, and he is working and been on his job for twelve years now, so we are making progress, or so I thought. Lately he has not been bringing the money home, and he is staying out later than usual. I need for you to help me get him back on track. What do I have to burn and light to get this husband of mine back on track? Signed, Not Having This

Answer 93: Dear Not Having This, what are you really asking me to do or help you do? Are you asking me to help you with the dark arts of occultism? Saltpeter does not work. I see you want me to help you control your husband through some external means to get him to become docile and compliant. Am I right?

What I think I am hearing is you want to see if I have in my bag of tricks some expertise of taking individuals' free will away. That is what I think I am hearing. Free will is every person on the planet's gift of choice. You would not want Infinite Spirit to empower you over your husband's God-given gift. I know it does not feel like a gift when you do not take the active use of choice.

If you feel compelled to misery, then you are using your choice. You cannot use your free will unless you are a child, and parents will not exhibit their free will from abuse. You have free will to shift this marriage of yours between you and your husband. It will not be through control; it will be through love and communication. There are symbols of love to ease in communication and open the understanding between the two of you, but you have to be willing to do your part in this marriage.

You must keep the lines of communication open and not involve your ego to taint the conversation because that is when your communication with your husband turns into a sea of angry, hateful words. Your husband is tired of the arguing, and you are throwing up what you have done for him, doing the time he was not working and was under the doctor's care. He is also tired of your children coming between the two of you. You have always financially rescued them whenever they use foolish and irresponsible behavior with their money.

He is tired of your excuses; that is why he will be dating another woman if this isn't rectified. Throw your ego out of the window and bring in compassion. Start from where you are—the present, not in the past. If you do not make up your mind to see the change and shift in your husband, the two of you will eventually be married to other people, and that road is paved with a lot of pain and turmoil.

Shift tools 93: You can get rid of anger and turmoil in the home with a long red dinner candle cut off the top and turned upside down so it can fit comfortably in a candleholder (you may have to cut off a good portion). Then dig up the wick from the opposite side and burn it. Say your favorite prayer of hope and love. You can even say, "*Help,*" as a prayer. Once done, light a fragrant white and pink candle for seven days.

You unify yourself with your vows of marriage and the Lord's prayer, and you should begin to see some results because lighting a candle is a way of extending one's prayer and showing solidarity with the person on whose behalf the prayer is offered; in this case, it is the union of this marriage.

Affirmation 93: I take time to get still and contemplate my blessings. I ask and I receive answers as I close my eyes and listen to the quiet voice within.

Issue 94: My Best Friend Has a Secret I Am Tired of Holding

My smart, intelligent best friend is married with three beautiful daughters, a husband who is hard working and is a dog at heart. His wife is also just as unfaithful. The couple lives in a beautiful suburb, and their children go to a great school. They have a housekeeper that comes into their home twice a week, which the housekeeper needs to come three times a week with all the laundry they have piled up and with their girl's busy schedule of events.

On the outside, my friend is a lesbian, and I am not only her best friend but her lover as well. I am also the godmother to two of her children. I have someone that is emotionally available and single like me, and I got to live my life out of the closet. I cannot see her anymore because her husband thinks she working late when she is with me.

Enough is enough with living this facade. She thinks no one is aware of our relationship when we are together. When I am with my other friends, I am automatically assumed that I am a lesbian, so I live my life "out," and my best friend lives her life "in." I think seventeen years of being in the shadows is enough. She has cheated on me in revenge for her husband being in compromising positions with her husband's business partners and friends.

My best friend and lover also had a past with a wealthy friend we have in common. That is too much to continue to deal with. She and her husband are bitter and painfully miserable with one another. They use horrible language in front of the girls, and they abuse the girls. The girls should have been taken away from them. In this case, the girls are very disrespectful to their parents. However, the oldest daughter is very respectful, and she tells me everything that goes on in that house, which, in my opinion, she should not know the dysfunction of her parents. I am leaving my best friend to her sad life, and I am moving to the sunshine of my life.

Answer 94: I hear you. You are leaving finally, again. I did not hear about how you are being loved and cherished. All that I am hearing is about your lover's life and her family dynamics. What happens when you are alone in your home? I'm not hearing how you operate.

It looks like you have a secret of not only being in love with a married woman but a secret from your own happiness because on the outside, your friend's life looks well put together with her husband and children. They appear to be living well as opposed to the "American dream" they appear to have it all. You, on the other hand, look frequently miserable.

This feels a little bitter, and you are placing yourself in a very comfortable seat of pain. Why? You are a spectator in her life as well as yours. When are you going to place your happiness in the forefront of your life like your life depended on it? (LOL) Sweetie, you deserve the best relationship that happiness has for you. Everything else is irrelevant. Your so-called lover is a user to the fifth degree.

Shift tools 94: Grab the brass ring of life for your full happiness. Step in the light of happiness, where the sunshine is filled with music and dance of life. You have been gone from yourself. (Listen to "Life is Ballad" by Abiah.) Come back into your own. Get back into your dancing. When I hear this song, I see you dancing and leaving the shadows of pain behind. (Also listen to "Goodbye" by Abiah.)

Affirmation 94: I am love, and I am really in the dance of love of life, and I never obscure myself from happiness.

INSIGHT WITHOUT CHANGE IS MEANINGLESS

Issue 95: My Son Is on the Floor

I just choked my thirteen-year-old son until he turned red. I had to stop and catch myself. I caught my son watching gay porn and in gay chat sites. My boyfriend has been telling me for months that my only child is gay. This boy has been telling my ex-husband that my boyfriend beat him because he does not want my boyfriend to tell my ex-husband our son is gay, which is not true. I am sending him to live with my ex-husband, his father. My boyfriend could lose his license to his limousine business dealing with my son. My boyfriend has packed his personal belongings to stay at his office until I come up with a solution. I do not have anything against gay people. I just do not want my son to be gay. I do not want to lose my boyfriend either. What is my solution?

Answer 95: This boy needs love and acceptance. Your boyfriend is right; your son is gay. Your son is not the butch gay teen. He is the femme gay teen complete with mascara and lip gloss. Your thirteen-year-old son has been on gay chat lines, exposing his pain regarding the divorce of his parents.

You have a new man in your life, and his father has a new woman in his life, and secretly your son was hoping the two of you would get back together to be a family again. Either way, you now know your son is gay. Your son's alternative lifestyle just would not have shown itself this early if you were still married. When mothers give birth to their babies, they are optimistic for these helpless little, tiny souls.

We get so easily disappointed when our will is not enforced, and we cannot mold these children the way we want them to be. Remember they come here with their complete minds and will of their own, living their very own path of life. Our role as parents is to prepare them to be the very best they can be in this world, to give them the tools to help them to discern from harmful situations and give them confidence to create a life for themselves where they can become whole, happy, complete, and productive individuals.

Shift tools 95: Allow your son his own path. Get support from parents-of-gay-teens organizations.

Affirmation 95: Today I allow my son his own experiences. I allow positive thoughts to fill and guide me moment by moment. I choose to be compassionate to my son, whom I love.

Issue 96: I Don't Want to Lose My Federal Express Job.

Hi, Ms. Dorothea. I was told to contact you regarding some injustices that are going on in my job. I've worked for Federal Express for twenty-two years and was reported for taking boxes of my truck during the December time frame. I have never done anything against my work ethics. In fact, I have a spotless work performance record and an excellent attendance record. Now I'm being investigated and sent home without pay until the investigation is over. Once it is over, I have to go in front of a board of managers to keep my job; this is wrong and injustice.

Answer 96: Don't worry. I see you think the worst while you worry. It's a habit which you need to get under control and reversed. I see there is a higher power intervening in keeping your job intact. All the lies will be revealed, and appropriate actions will be taken. Your character is well spoken, and your tenure will stay in place. You will return to your job. There may be some micromanaging going on, and that is due to your worry and negative thinking. Relax.

Shift tools 96: Release the anxiety. Repeat the Lord's prayer three times a day, every day. Try to see what you really want as opposed to what you do not want. Reverse all that you say that is negative and speak the opposite, which is positive.

Affirmation 96: My job is safe and secure. Thy will be done. I am happy, healthy, wealthy, and wise.

Issue 97: Child Support

I don't understand why child-support court can't catch my lowlife husband. Every six months it looks like he is driving a new vehicle. (Seething.) He always is seen around town at the local night spots, showing off, spending money, and showing off his new clothes and shoes every day. He has the latest two expensive phones, the latest gadgets that are in existence, and his girlfriend is jewelry down and wearing oh-so-nice clothing.

She has the latest gadgets and gear as well. I keep hearing how he is traveling and taking trips to Jamaica, St. Croix, Dominican Republic, and he cannot pay his child support for his son. What the f——ck. I'm am so tired of seeing him parading around town and doing nothing for his flesh-and-blood child. When is he going to get what's coming to him because? As far as I am concerned, he keeps landing on his feet. Nothing detrimental is happening to him.

Answer 97: I know this is painful, and it seems from your eyes this is unfair and unjust. Your ex-husband is getting more attention than ever before. That is what happens when you write a song, and it is a hit, and the artist who sings it is making the writer famous. Your ex-husband thought and wanted to share his success with you. His desire was to share this life with you until he caught you in bed with his so-called best friend.

Why did you have to get revenge? Getting even is a sticky web we spin out of control. Your husband was caught with a stripper on camera nineteen months ago, and you never forgave him. Now he is famous; this is a surprise to you because while you were married, he could not get any of his lyrics looked at all. He grew so miserable while working in that car wash, and he felt you didn't care as long as he brought some money in the home.

You didn't support his dream because you didn't believe in his dream, and you told him on more than one occasion that he was wasting his time. When that situation happened with his friend, that divorce took place quickly, and a proper child support wasn't in place because you thought the best friend and you would be together. As you can see, that was not the case.

Shift tools 97: To heal this discord fast, write a forgiveness letter. To do the forgiveness opens blessings for you. Forgive yourself.

Affirmation 97: I stand in the healing light of love and allow love to permeate me, and every cell of my body is absorbed in love and forgiveness.

Issue 98: I'm Am Not Supported, I'm

Always There for Everybody

I am tired of being the Rock of Gibraltar for everyone around me. No one cares enough about me to pick up the phone to call and see how I am doing. My husband ignores me and has nothing but mean comments to say to me. I help and nurse everybody back to wellness in my family. When my mother was dying of cancer, I had to return home and help put everything in order despite all my siblings still living in the same town as my mother, and one lives two doors down the street.

When I get sick and when I am in the hospital, nobody is around to help me to recovery, including my husband, who

INSIGHT WITHOUT CHANGE IS MEANINGLESS

is a big asshole with two holes! The doctor called me and told me about my scheduled impending surgery. When I informed my husband what the doctor said and the type of surgery I had to have, my husband, Gerald, said he could not take me, but he will call a cab to take me to the hospital. Afterward he would meet me later because he has two meetings he could not miss.

I'm reflecting when his aunt, who raised him, didn't like me at all when she was dying for the fifth and seventh time, and she never went anywhere. I was at her bedside, cleaning, preparing meals, washing clothes, and making sure she had taken her medication. While he was in the den of his aunt's home, talking to coworkers (supposedly) about project mergers.

In the meantime, sweat was dripping off my forehead since his two-hundred-pound aunt never cleaned her house. This was a usual occurrence every time she was about to die. I get so angry after reflecting on all the maid services I've given for his aunt. My ungrateful husband wouldn't get off his high horse and help me with anything. He doesn't behave like a partner, but acts like a visitor in this marriage. What am I going to do? We've been married twenty-three years. (Crying.) Nobody cares about me. I'm so alone and lonely (crying).

Answer 98: The part of your marriage vows that said in sickness and in health seems to be the big focus of your life. What steps have you taken to put yourself first? Do not say you cannot because everybody needs you. You have not talked about any hobbies or interests outside your marriage that you are interested in.

What groups or organizations do you belong to? What church are you affiliated with? Have you put your family tree or your husband's family tree together? This will fill up your days with research and a deep sense of satisfaction. Have you picked up some of those talents you were interested in high school and college? What about writing workshops and other types of workshops that will increase the talent you already have?

Do not focus on where you are. Focus on who you are—that is, an enormously incredible talented person that has so much to share with the world. People in the world would gain so much from your grace and presence, which is a gift. You may need to get a life coach to help you shift perspective. That feeling of loneliness will all but disappear.

Shift tools 98: Life coach—research for one that will meet your needs. Take steps to get involved in the million and one activities this world or your town has to offer. You are a viable visible person and soon will attract viable, visible, loving new friends to you.

Affirmation 98: I am more than a nursemaid. Today I communicate with an open heart of love and joy, and I refrain from nonproductive communication.

Issue 99: Should I Keep This Pregnancy or Not?

Hi, Ms. Dorothea. My fiancée and I bought a beautiful home together five years ago. We talked about planning our wedding but are now separated. Our separation was due to many disagreements. Do you, Ms. Dorothea, foresee us getting back together, and should I keep this pregnancy? He doesn't know.

Answer 99: Well, I see your hormones are hard at work. I do not know how he does not know you are pregnant with all the complaining and insults you have been lashing out at him. To answer your question, yeah, I can see that. (Whew) Yes, for the questions, he is returning because he loves you, so ease up a little, little momma. Your moods will not stay fluctuated like this for much longer. You love him, you know him, and you want him, so have his baby.

INSIGHT WITHOUT CHANGE IS MEANINGLESS

Shift tools 99: Place self in his shoes, and he does not understand why you are a ball of knot. Practice compassion.

Affirmation 99: Life is full of ups and downs. I dig for compassion and gratitude, which are parts of me as a whole. I embrace the love of my fiancée.

Issue 100: When Is My Crazy Tenant Leaving?

I hired a property-management company to manage my (one) rental property and place tenants in my rental home. This management company has a great reputation for placing the ideal person in a property because of their extensive background checks.

In my case, the management company put in a paranoid schizophrenic with arson tendency, and he comes from a wealthy family. Instead of doing a thorough background check on the tenant, which is their policy, the six months' rent in advance was all the background check they needed. The second month of the tenant's stay, the property manager wanted to get into my rental home to check for fire extinguishers, and the tenant acted like the SWAT team was trying break down the doors with a battering ram.

The five-feet-two-inch, 120 lbs. blonde with brown roots female property manager rang the doorbell and knocked to gain access. She asked to enter the house to check the fire extinguishers for his safety because of the reminder from the local fire department. The fire department was filling extinguishers as a courtesy. The tenant screamed at the top of his lungs with all sorts of profanity of how he was not going to enter the house with the old fire-extinguisher trick. She started to bang on the door from the other side, and he told her to get the hell off his property. Frightened, the property manager quickly left the property.

The fourth month the police have been getting constant threats that the tenant in my property has been terrorizing the neighbors and threatening them with terroristic threats to keep them from looking in his windows at night, which was imaginary. The property manager tried to talk to him, and this time she was successful. He returned her call, and she was allowed to come into the rental property. He looked as if he lived there seven years. It was filled to the rim with furniture, papers, firearms, and newspapers from front to back; paint cans, wall hangings, and other contraptions.

When the property manager entered the house, her eyes widened because of the unexpected, but she maintained her composure. The tenant acted gracious and normal, since he didn't understand the neighbors' complaints because he kept to himself. If strangers came on his property without permission or uninvited, he had a right to protect himself. His family paid the additional six months' rent. He began to feel unwanted because the property manager inquired too much. He was threatening to break the lease and move, which would've been a relief. However, he continued to stay there, making the neighbors miserable.

The next-door neighbor didn't want to leave his wife home alone because of the tenant's unpredictability. The neighbor felt as though they were seized in their own home. Every time someone would walk outside to enter their car, the tenant would come outside and swear at my old neighbors.

They finally called me, and I called the property manager that I hired to get some information on the tenant that was placed on my property. I searched his name, and in no time a whole stack of problems came up with him and previous neighborhoods and subdivisions; this wasn't his first time terrorizing a neighborhood. They told me no background check was performed at all.

INSIGHT WITHOUT CHANGE IS MEANINGLESS

The only "check" performed was given to the property manager, along with her commission. The tenant's background was overlooked, and there was no background investigation to see if he would be a perfect fit. My question to you is, when is this tenant moving out? He makes threats weekly that he is moving. Will he?

Answer 100: My answer to you is, no. You would have to get an act from Congress to get him out of there before his lease is up despite his phony threats, along with several moving trucks to haul his belongings and debris from your rental home, which I see, will take additional time.

Shift tools 100: Relax, release anger, and stop watching the calendar. Take long walks and allow management to handle what they got themselves into.

Affirmation 100: As I do activities that bring me joy and happiness, I have fun and enjoy all of life's pleasures and outcomes.

Issue 101: What Kind of Life Will My Autistic Daughter Have?

Ms. Dorothea, I love my little girl, and she has been diagnosed with Autism and is high functioning.

Answer 101: Your autistic daughter will have a full, well-rounded life. I see there are many levels of autism, and your daughter's disability is mild. She interacts well with people. She makes pulling gestures to herself, along with the ticks and self-talking alone; but I see when people are interacting with her, she speaks and gives eye contact.

As she gets older, the autism will almost be undetectable. She will appear as everyone else with a light avant-garde appeal, or a person who dances to the beat of her own drum, but she assimilates well too. Her behavior merges into an independent, removed, and social when she wants to be, which balances itself out. She is not emotionally attached to anything insecure. She will be educated and protected by her social circle, so you don't have to worry your daughter; she won't be a target for unsavory characters. She is unique and not a clone of an awesome, artistic young person that has a lot to offer the world.

Shift 101: Practice seeing only the best for her. Speak, think, and write all the positive you want for her. Script this in a journal and write about it daily until you see it seamlessly.

Affirmation 101: God has a wonderful paint pallet, placed so many beautiful human canvasses that adds beauty and character to the world in which heals and fills all the fragmented colorless cracks and crevices of pain in the world. My daughter is that beauty added to heal and be loved and give a bouquet of love to the world.

Issue 102: I Feel I Went Too Far to Spice Up My Marriage

Dorothea, usually every day I talk to a really good friend of mine. So on this particular day, I am going to say in the spring, this good friend of mine and I was talking. In the conversation, she said something about a threesome she had in college and a few years ago (now we've been out of college for a few years—at least twenty years, I would say, so you know how old we are). She said she had one many years ago (hump, I was thinking). It was an experience, which did a lot for her relationship at that time.

Well, it got me thinking, and *bim, bam, boom,* I discussed it with my husband, and he was surprisingly happy and was willing to try it; and we decided to go through with it, and he thought it would be with my friend, which was out of the question. We had always had a mutual friend named Dawn that we knew we could approach with this idea, and she said, "Yes, sounds like fun."

One evening we got together, and it was a foursome, not a threesome. So that was okay. We had ambiance, wine, and one thing led to another. My husband was very comfortable, and I couldn't get comfortable, so I didn't participate. I made excuses to leave the house while my friend's boyfriend (AJ) followed me. We sat at Starbucks until closing just talking. He understood, and I was relieved to not go through with it because AJ didn't want Dawn, my friend, to see how much he liked me. AJ was a good friend to me that night. I took spice to the danger zone. I wished I had not ventured down this road.

My husband appeared to enjoy himself since I gave him permission to cheat. Now I can't rid myself of this feeling that the two of them are still seeing each other. So, Ms. Dorothea, is it true? Are they still seeing each other? This is my big question. D. Rue

Answer 101: Yes, they are still seeing each other, and her boyfriend can confirm it, though he may not want to confirm it. I am surprised you did not ask AJ.

In addition to what I am seeing, and I wonder if AJ would confirm this, your husband looks like he wants a threesome with a woman and another man. AJ may not be the one, but I am sure your husband would not mind if it was AJ. Stop beating up on yourself; it is time to seek solutions to release this night affair. It is time to talk to your friendly counselor to start the process of resolving.

God has not forsaken you nor are you being punished. Put prayer work in motion and stop acting as though you're the worst woman in the world. All things can begin to go into place through prayer, and you are a faithful woman that just got caught up. In the scheme of fifty years of marriage, which is coming, this incident is the easiest and funniest to handle in the years to come.

Shift tools 101: Get still and ask yourself, do you want your marriage? Then take steps to shift. Forgive yourself for this phase of your marriage. Look and read *The Twelve Steps to Forgiveness.* Talk to your husband and have some resources lined up instead of finger-pointing and screaming.

Affirmation 101: I am not forsaken, and I am not judged.

Issue 102: My Sister Sued My Homeowner's Insurance

I can't believe my sister sued my homeowner's insurance because she fell down my basement stairs. For one, her old ass wore heels that were too high; that was why she slipped her big butt down the stairs. Now she hurt her ankles, hips, and back, and she wants my insurance to pay for her medical bills. My family is awful. Should I countersue her?

Answer 102: Breathe deeply. I see this is going to be a big split decision with the family, who's going to take who's side. I know you don't care. She is going to sue and get her bills paid, and you will countersue in small claims court and will not win. You should insist your sister take her shoes off in your home.

Shift tools 102: You really need to have some deep talks with your pastor and consider some meditation classes. If you shift, your sister shifts too.

Affirmation 102: I am open to change and looking at things from another person's point of view.

Issue 103: My Husband and I Are Separated

Dear Dorothea, my husband and I are separated due to him being an abuser of alcohol and marijuana. I am not a prude.

I am all for having a good time, and I didn't mind that he indulged due to the fact his job was hectic and stressful. He worked with mutual funds and helping people work with their incomes at the financial institution where he works.

To tell you the truth, he came into my life when I wasn't truly where I needed to be in my career, and he was a wonderful distraction; but now I got myself back together, and I own a very successful boutique in the Atlanta area. I am forever grateful for my husband, but now that we are separated, I am really ready to move forward in my life. He has been trying to get back into my good graces, and he plays The Flamingos song, "I Only Have Eyes for You." I would melt every time that song played, which was always by his request because you know that song isn't played anywhere.

However, it was playing when I met him in a pool joint in Atlanta, and our eyes met. I am stronger and not so nostalgic, and to tell you the truth, I am doing much better without him. He was helping me with my business, and I see some fatal flaws in his management. We have been married seven years, and I am tired especially when the police stopped him for drunk-driving and drove him home to me.

The police officer asked me a scenario of questions and basically told me he didn't know what's wrong with my husband as he (police officer) said, "You are beautiful [at 4:00 a.m.] and being startled out of your sleep. You look absolutely radiant." The officer continued to say, "You should have seen the things [woman] he was talking to. She looked like a drag queen learning to put on makeup, and your husband was all over her in the car. I stopped your husband from swerving uncontrollably on the road."

The police officer followed and allowed the passenger to drive and drop off the car at our home at my husband's insistence. According to the officer, my husband also wanted the officer to let his wife (me) know where he would be, which is in the county jail. This was highly unheard of, but the officer was so kind, and that incident gave me the strength to drop off most of my husband's things to his parents and let them know where he was—in the county jail for driving under the influence.

When I told his parents, their mouths dropped open as they were heading to church. My in-laws think their son is pure as the driven snow and that they did not know he ever drank a drop of alcohol, and that's been because of me. Now they know. Can you believe it? This thirty-four-year-old man, their son, which they didn't know at all drinks; my in-laws pretty much thought I was hell's spawn that corrupted their baby (this grown man). Well, mainly my mother-in-law and I remained respectful even now. And another thing, my husband didn't satisfy me sexually like all my boyfriends before him. When he indulged, it was a travesty in bed. I stayed because of my vows. Do you think I am acting too hasty, or should I just throw in the towel? Loleen H.

Answer 103: (Chuckling to myself) Dear Loleen (whew), you said a mouthful, and I am not hearing something. Something big has been left out of the question or the dissertation of events. I would like to go back to what the police officer said to you, "You look so radiant at 4:00 a.m.," when you got the knock on your door. I am assuming, but who were you talking to? Because I am sensing you were not sleeping during this time of the 4:00 a.m. knock at your door.

You seem pretty alert not for just a phone call but could you have been Skyping with someone else for the fact you were looking so radiant? I'm feeling exhilaration in your throat and loins (LOL), while you could lounge, relax, and speak freely alone. Since your husband was out, and the deep voice on the other end of the phone or computer monitor

INSIGHT WITHOUT CHANGE IS MEANINGLESS

screen appears to be able to coax you away for the weekend. In addition, you had a hard time figuring out what lie to tell your husband to substantiate this getaway (LOL).

Now, problem solved. You can go freely and enjoy the company of the deep voice (huggy bear) you have been Skyping with. You know you have been looking forward to this day (not quite this outcome, but nonetheless). Who wouldn't want a long weekend in Destin, Florida? True your husband has been cheating, which I do not understand why you did not notice him leaving the room every time he got a call; those were not all business calls. I see your friends noticed. Do you feel guilty for introducing him to the variety of marijuana and indulging with him in the privacy of your home? Maybe, but your husband's paranoia is monumental, almost frightening.

Since he is a drinker (I am not going to say "typical Scorpio," but I was thinking it) long before you met him and a big drinker at that, you will now hear all the dirt from friends and acquaintances that they viewed your husband on many occasions drunk inside and outside the club. Sometimes they didn't know how he made it home on those nights. Most of the time the friends assumed you picked him up, which I don't understand that since the two of you only had one vehicle.

You know this firsthand when you go out, you have to drive home, and to get the keys from your husband is always a long debate until you started carrying a spare set of keys. You have a high tolerance and rarely appear intoxicated if ever in public. But your real question is, should you stay or leave, since your husband financially is failing and then sex is so much better alone, when he isn't in the equation?

I'm not sure what the question is, but the bottom line is, you have not been happy with your marriage. Your business has fallen off, and your husband's pay has fallen off as well. Finally, he doesn't rock your world in bed because of being too high, drunk, or just not endowed enough. Let's not forget his cheating and your emotional cheating. To me, that is it pretty much in a nutshell.

Shift tools 103: Guilt and failure, in this case, is useless. Begin to take steps to breathe often and write out a plan of attack to get back on your feet with your business, yourself, and marriage. Put it in perspective and see which direction you can get help to bring up back into the functioning businesswoman. Look in the mirror and start loving what you see. Laugh, jump, and dance in that mirror. Turn on music and begin the process of healing.

Affirmation 103: I am a soul having many human experiences, and I love and accept me. I take action in living my fullest life, and I reach out and take all that life has to offer.

Issue 104: Where Are the Enlightened Men That Are Straight?

Hi, Dorothea. I have a hard time being on this spiritual journey single. It has been an experience to become more aware. I love this spiritual path that I'm on and wouldn't change the choice of enlightenment. I am learning so much about myself and understanding forgiveness, positive thinking, setting my intentions, along with how my thoughts are such a creative force. This has been so healing for me. I meditate morning and night, I eat healthily, and I keep my temple beautiful. I would like to be on this journey with some like-minded gentleman as well. To be on such a wonderful journey and the thought of being alone is daunting but not deterring. I know there are men out there that have done work on themselves. Your thoughts? Asheena M.

INSIGHT WITHOUT CHANGE IS MEANINGLESS

Answer 104: Yes, yes, this is a popular topic, believe it or not. Many women that are on this journey as yourself have come to me with this question and/or topic. Asheena, many of the wonderful men that appear to have the same understanding of this journey and follow it seem to play for the other team (as it has been explained to me) and the other men are fanatical, obsessive, or creepy.

This is what has been told to me. My response has been, as you well know is, let's set the intentions on what it is you want in your life. To set your intention, you must get still and know what you want. Then get focus and write and/or meditate on what you want. I script usually and meditate on what I want. Asheena, to script, you write in present tense what you want as though it is happening, and it's usually in the form of gratitude and staying focused on the presence, griping not. Watch your expectations take shape.

Shift tools 104: Think about the positive attributes of others today. Realizing negative thoughts will, in the end, hurt your soul. Take a positive approach in knowing what resonates with you. Positive thinking, no griping or complaining, and speak into existence what you really want.

Okay, if you do not know how to do this, then start with writing down what you don't want. Look at the things you wrote down and then write the opposite. Talk with like-minded individuals. Look in a mirror often and affirm what you want in the present tense. Visualize your right, perfect partner loving you and being a part of this journey of Christ consciousness. See you and him working in your spiritual community, volunteering and growing strong spiritually.

Affirmation 104: (Looking in a mirror) Today I release the past and step into the miracle of now, which has brought me my right and perfect love in my life, and we are excited to enjoy a future of love and happiness.

Issue 105: I Want My Boyfriend to Marry Me—What Am I Doing Wrong?

Hey, Ms. Dorothea. My name is Mandy, short for Amanda. I've been with my boyfriend for two years and nine months, and I love him very much and his son who lives with him every other weekend. I stay with my parents. It looks like I may have to get my own place to live, since my boyfriend hasn't asked me to marry him. I told him I wanted the whole package for better or worse, in sickness and health, etc. He says I have a temper, and I am crazy because I told him to stop going out of his way, pissing me off, and trying to make me jealous.

We broke up a couple of times, and it didn't last long; we ultimately got back together. I've done a few things I'm ashamed of, which made me totally out of line, but at the time I felt there was no recourse to do what I felt instinctual. I do feel a factor in our relationship not growing. It's his two friends that do not like me. My boyfriend is swayed by their opinion, and in turn, when they are around, that's when we have our worst difficulties. When they are not around, we are beautifully happy. How can I convince my boyfriend to marry me? Thank you. Mandy.

Answer 105: Mandy, you cannot convince your boyfriend to marry you because he is tired of you. It appears the only reason the two of you get back together is that you initiated the getting back together. I see your boyfriend is used to the two of you being together, but he has grown tired and weary of you and all the antics you put him through.

His friend has said they don't know what he sees in you because you have put him through hell, and they don't understand why he still puts up with you. His friends put a wager out that they think you're going to burn down his house, and that's when your boyfriend will get the wake-up call to finally get rid of you. Plus, your boyfriend's friends' girlfriends don't like you either. I would say you two need a hiatus from one another, but he won't take you back if you do. It is time for you to assess where this relationship is going and if it is worth you continuing it. He is not going to marry you in this lifetime. I do see each of you marrying other people. So yes, you will get married, to another boyfriend.

Shift tools 105: Sit quietly and breathe in deeply fifty times.

Issue 106: When Will I Get a Girlfriend?

Ms. Dorothea, I am a twenty-three-year-old healthy heterosexual male who's in college, and I work a job to pay for my apartment and other expenses that may occur. I have never had a girlfriend. I talk to girls all the time at work, school, at restaurants, and wherever I am in my travels per day. I am not afraid of conversing with women. I just don't find a lot of women take me seriously.

When I was in high school, a lot of girls would come up to me to talk just to give me a compliment. Now that I am in the real world, it's a little different. They talk to me, but the topic is always about how to make their relationship with their boyfriends better. I have become the resident counselor on how to keep a boyfriend, and I have never had a girlfriend. I thought it was because I did not have a car. I don't want to take a woman out on the bus, but my roommates didn't have a car and managed to get many women. Hell, they got women with cars. Now they have cars of their own, and it's probably much easier for them, but initially, that was not the case. What is wrong with this scenario?

Answer 106: It appears you're a caring young man that really respects and understands the needs of young women.

The girls dating your friends seem to think so, and some of these girls have said to their boyfriends they should be more like you.

The problem is you. You're on the fence about having a girlfriend, it seems. You feel you don't have a healthy financial income to have a girlfriend. You also feel you cannot impress a girl if you're not driving a vehicle of your own. I see you do have a driver's license. You will be driving your own vehicle in less than a few months. I see your diligence will pay off. Your thoughts keep you stifled because you overthink too much. Your competing thoughts won't allow you to see past your roommate's accomplishments or the guys around you that have succeeded in getting cars. You are doing well, working your way through school, though it is not easy for you, and it appears you have to put in more time than the average student to study while relistening to the taped lectures from your professors.

On top of your busy schedule, you cannot and do not try to fit women in your life unless it just platonic. You appear to have a lot of platonic relationships with young women and you all are just fine with that connection. I don't see these young women pushing the issue to be exclusive with you, and it seems you wouldn't mind if one or two of them did, since the women around you are aggressive with everyone else but you.

What I am getting at is, you are a little different from your male counterparts—meaning, you are a soulful, sensitive kind of guy with no panache, no Rico Suave, no swagger. What I am trying to say is, you're no Gentleman Quarterly example (GQ). C'mon, you're working a decent job; a weekly haircut should fit in your schedule. Is that so difficult to do? Haircuts are not just for when you have plans to go somewhere. Your head is being looked at daily not only when you have plans.

INSIGHT WITHOUT CHANGE IS MEANINGLESS

Women don't want to look at an ungroomed guy all the time or anytime. Who wants to be with that type of guy? Will that make a wonderful impression with friends and family, bringing home an ungroomed guy?

When you look ungroomed, you also look unsanitary, dirty, and unwashed, as though you just awakened and picked up your books from the floor, or you may have walked outside, bypassing the bathroom altogether. You are a conversationalist, and you do not mind sharing your thoughts, ideas, and philosophy, which I think is great. However, women are looking at you hard while you're talking and silently critiquing you, and your teeth is a major concern. You should get white strips, keep a toothbrush on you, and keep your lips moisturized. Chapped lips are such a turn-off. Grooming has been your number one problem since you left your mother's home.

Now that you are on your own, your appearance looks unwashed, and your clothes look too snug. When you were in high school, you dressed as though you were born with a silver spoon in your mouth. Your friends were always complimenting you on your gear and trying to copy your style; even the teachers loved your style correction (your mother's style).

Well, now you are a grown man whose gotten his independence, and your mother has zero input in your style of dress or anything, and that's the way you want it. Okay, that's cool and all, but what is your style? Is it that "just rolled out of DORITOS crumbs with pizza-crust crumbs clinging to your clothes and face at the same time while you are looking at beautiful women"? Tell me what part of that style is attractive. Spraying body spray on an unwashed body will not do the trick either (despite the commercials).

Look, there are too many wonderful examples of males in the world that are dapper, rugged, cool, sophisticated, preppy, and fresh, and so clean-clean (Outkast), or the boy-next-door look. I am not saying you should follow any of those examples, but coming from a place of impeccable dressing, including your footwear matching your clothing as well, your mother kept you looking wonderful and unique.

Now from that spectrum to almost looking like everything you wear comes from a place called hand-me-down junction. You may have a much more conservative flare than your mom, and you want to just be independent, thinking and dressing. The reason girls seek you out for advice is that you're more laid-back than your roommates and friends. The girls liked that testosterone didn't rule you.

Basically, you think first and act later. With a lot of girls, that is an impressive trait. Okay, listen. I am not saying you have to be superficial and wear the finest in clothing; that is not it. Be *clean*, look *clean*, smell clean, and wear clothes that fit. Conservative is not a dirty word, but funky is. Women love confident, well-groomed men regardless of style and dress. Do not get me or hear me wrong. Style of dress is important, coupled with being well groomed, charisma, and confidence; you will win every time.

Shift tools 106: Invest more time into basic grooming. What male figures do you admire whose philosophy and demeanor is much like yours? (Emulate some to get a feel of how you would like to look.) Get a stylist. There are many young people going to school for fashion and style design all around you. Seek out these individuals, and it will not be hard. In this age of social media, you are sure to find the right and perfect (student) person for you. That person will help you find a style all your own.

Leave your overbloated ego at home with the DORITOS chip crumbs and half-eaten paraphernalia on your floor because feeling like you don't need help and that a stranger can't tell you what to wear will keep you from getting the quality girlfriend you want. Stream *Hitch*, the movie, or rent it. (I'm not placing you in any character role. I just want you to know when you need help, help is available.)

Affirmation 106: Today is the perfect day to start investing in me. I make wonderful impressions with style all my own. I am complimented often, and people love being in my company. Friends flock to me, and invitations to the best and latest functions are always in full throttle.

Issue 107: What Is She Thinking, I Don't Have Bills to Pay?

Hi, Ms. Dorothea. I would like your view on my situation because I'm ready to be blunt with her. I have allowed this friend of mine to get on her feet. She left her husband for the third time, my longtime friend who is staying with me, along with her teenage daughter that dropped out of school and went back to school and got her GED.

Now she wants to go to school to be a fashion designer, but she wants to pursue being with a derelict guy. She calls her boyfriend, who is a thief and a marijuana-smoking broke bit——. Apparently, my longtime friend's daughter has been spending many days and nights at the marijuana boyfriend's place because his mother is a substance abuser and doesn't stay in the home for long periods at a time. My job has given me a lot of leniencies, and I have been able to get people to work for short periods at a time.

So my friend got a few little contract positions with my company. Well, I've been laid off or fired, whichever word you choose to use. I got some lousy compensation, and now I need help more than ever. In the beginning, my friend said she will look for a job, then her car broke down, so I helped her with a job here and there. I helped her, but I wanted her and her daughter to help themselves by actively looking for stable employment.

The daughter was going to be registered for school, which happened, and she didn't go to one class. Then she found out she was pregnant with triplets. This happened in spite of my warnings and practically begging for two years for her to get on her feet and leave her daughter with her ex-husband because he is a better parent. Another thing, women are paying out the nose for invitro fertility to get twins, triplets, or just one healthy baby, and this child (*ho*) laid up with her legs wide open and got triplets with no problem, no job, no home, no money, no boyfriend support, and no education.

So how is this child going to survive? Enough said on that note. Her mother knew that outcome because it was spoken by me. When is this woman getting out of my house and working at a normal job of any sort? She is now going to school online and using even more of my gas, electricity, water, and food because she eats all day long. If she was working and going to a physical building to a school, she would be utilizing the school's library and cafeteria and paying for meals with the money she earned from her employment. I know I sound like a horrible friend, but it has been a little over a year, and I have gotten rent from her maybe once. I am ready to get my life back. LSW.

Answer 107: Hello, Miss LSW, whew, I feel your exhaustion and guilt. On one hand, you want to be there for your friend, and on the other hand, you can't believe your friend will take advantage of you. To be down and out is one thing, and then bringing company along to help make a desperate situation even more intolerable can appear to be taking your kindness for weakness.

Your friend's daughter, who appears to be an adult since she does everything an adult does, she didn't want to stay with her dad because Dad has rules, and Mom doesn't; and if Mom did have rules, who cares? because nobody listens to Mom aka your longtime friend, and this is from her daughter's perspective. Your longtime friend is lazy and does not want to be bored, so anything that sounds structured and traditional, she does not want to do that kind of work. That's what was so great about the little contract positions you gave her; it was fun, quick, and she got to be around some pretty influential people, so that was worth her while.

Your longtime friend has a dependent nature, like her family she comes from. It looks like the women in her family are dependent in many ways because of the matriarch in the family. The grandmother was not a milk-and-cookies grandmother, more like the Ma Barker type. She ruled with an iron fist and could make her daughters do whatever it took to survive and get what they wanted, short of being a Lady of the Night but anything else, so your friend would really have to fight some of these family traits, which are based in fear.

Your friend has a fear of not accomplishing success and a fear of having to be dependent on her biological family and knowing they will never help her. She is used to being abandoned by her family; her resentment toward them is generating an environment within her, which she's becoming the very thing she resents at your expense. She comes from people who will think it nothing to swindle or take advantage of anyone or anything.

Now, your friend does not display this personality—it is subtle and laced with embarrassment—so she clings to you out of friendship and knowing your personality for helping people. The one thing you have been doing is boiling with your own resentment at yourself and at your longtime friend.

I suggest you and she sit down and discuss timing; graciously ask her how much longer she plans on staying with you and how you can help her execute a plan to be in her own space so she can feel free and more comfortable. I see your longtime friend responding well because coming from a place of graciousness, she does not feel defensive and is willing to talk to you in order to receive help in becoming more independent.

Shift tools 107: You do not like being taken advantage of. You are an excellent communicator of what you want directly. Your life is important. Put yourself first and start enjoying the company of so many other people that want to be with you. Release responsibility. Release the guilt. Release the contract. No one disintegrates because you want your life back.

Affirmation 107: I teach like Jesus taught: teach to fish, give advice, not my life.

Response from the Questioners

Questioner 2 Has Responded

Yes, Ms. Dorothea, with reluctance I've done the exercises you suggested, which seem so simple, too simple, to get a life of happiness. The affirmation was rather long, but it worked. I felt a shift. I am at an age that I now realize having children is out of the question because I am forty and past childbearing age. I want a partner, a life partner to share my life with, to travel, and to set in motion wonderful memories. I love traveling abroad. I am tired of traveling with groups of strangers that I do not seem to gel with and girlfriends who talk about their husbands and children on the whole trip. I am ready for someone who has the same loves in common as I.

Okay, I did the stretching exercises, breathing deeply and releasing, quieting my mind, and presently getting still to start connecting to invisible higher power. It felt all powerful. I kept

INSIGHT WITHOUT CHANGE IS MEANINGLESS

hearing your voice in some of my meditations, saying, "Move into the place of my greatness. That space is an empty move into place." I kept trying to figure out where that space was, and all it was is a shift in believing I had a space of greatness; and like magic, it felt like I heard a click in the far distance. I could feel worries known and unknown lifting from my presence.

I now feel wonderful and light. I am proud to say I met a man name Jonathan, a very successful even-natured CFO who's been to self-improvement counselors for the last ten years. Jonathan does qigong daily; he has taught me the technique, and it has helped me with my anxiety and meditations. Jonathan meditates and focuses on what he puts into his body, and he eats food that nourishes as well as heal, which has helped me to stay motivated on how I prepare meals.

We have many of the same interests. I see the growth in myself, and he has said the same about himself. I like him a lot, and I would like to see where this takes us. Thank you, Dorothea, for opening my eyes. I see the change, and Johnathan is very different from any guy I've ever met and dated. A shift had taken place.

Question 6 Has Responded

You are right, Ms. Dorothea, on so many levels. I feel and look young but understand I don't get a do-over. Those years are gone. I am and have been exploring the real true interest that I haven't been able to cultivate while thoroughly taking care of my family needs. I love art, and I am ready to reinvent myself as an art curator or work with private art auctions and galleries. I am happy and ready to live in the now and enjoy the wisdom I have with all its exciting nuances.

My husband and I renewed our vows and took a second honeymoon. Wow, it was wonderful to hear him call me his young bride. Onlookers watched our vows renewed and thought I was my husband's second wife. You could hear the gasp at telling them we had been married twenty-five years, and this was our second honeymoon. Something lifted and melted away as I rededicated myself to my husband. Thank you, Dorothea, for helping me see the light.

Questioner 7 Has Responded

Ms. Dorothea, one day I was feeling low, and I went to the grocery store because I needed to get out of the house. I drove and drove and found myself in another area because I was thinking so much. I drove right out of my neighborhood. I saw what I thought was my local grocery store. For a quick moment I forgot I wasn't in my nearby store.

There was a coffee shop in this store, and it smelled so good, so I sat down in the coffee area to get a large coffee. I noticed the interior was much more modern than what I was used to; a culinary chef was in the hot-food section, which looked like an upscale eatery. I marveled at the differences. It took my mind off my troubles at home. The coffee was good, and it felt good to be away from home in a state of frustration.

I know this sounds cliché, but a man walked past me and backed up to ask me about avocados; he wanted to make guacamole with a hard avocado. I laughed and told him he would have to wait until that particular avocado softened, or he would have to go back to produce and get a much-softer avocado. He complimented my smile. He asked to sit down, and we began talking. Before we knew it, the loudspeaker said it was ten minutes to closing and to bring purchases to the register.

Yes, five hours went by, and the gentleman was barely able to get his purchases in. I bought a few items nowhere near

INSIGHT WITHOUT CHANGE IS MEANINGLESS

what I was supposed to pick up. The lights were going out, and we walked out of the store, and he walked me to my car, and he gave me his number. He told me he really enjoyed our conversation and hoped to speak to me again, being respectful to my boyfriend. He said he did not want to cause trouble in my current situation. If I chose to talk, I would have his number.

Up to now, my boyfriend and I haven't had in-depth conversations like the one I had with this man in the store—never ever—and this made me think seriously about why I was desperately holding on to my boyfriend. Do I value the years and history we had, or am I afraid of going through the duplicate hardships I had with him in a new guy, with additional difficulties I don't yet know about? Am I sticking with the fool I know as opposed to a new fool I do not know?

That five-hour conversation I had with the man in the grocery store felt right. I have these types of conversations with my girlfriends with less flirtation, but real conversations. What an eye-opener. The conversations with my boyfriend left me drained, tired, and frustrated. I felt high on happiness; it left me wanting more kinds of conversations like that. My family and friends have been telling me how beautiful I am, and I have so much to offer a man who will reciprocate it.

This day is really the first day I sunk in the pain of unsatisfaction from deep, unfulfilled love. I sobbed so hard, not cry, sobbed; it felt like layers of my soul was being lifted, and for the first time, I felt foolish, stupid, and ashamed that I felt low, low, and ashamed. I have been trying to make a man be with me that obviously loathes me and is using me for a place to stay. Why couldn't I let him go? Dorothea, you gave me the truth, and I did not want to face it. I did not book a single cruise. The grocery store was proof enough that I was desirable and that men do communicate.

About the Author

Dorothea has worked in the field of clairvoyant life-coaching for over twenty-five years. She has helped a number of people heal, make better decisions and receive a better outcome to their dilemmas than what would have happened without her advice. Dorothea has a gift for giving insight and tools to help end chronic dissatisfaction and have the life and outcome they truly want.

Dorothea has been a Clairvoyant featured locally on radio shows in Atlanta, Georgia; Macon, Georgia; Jackson, Mississippi; Florida; and Cincinnati, Ohio and has been on a syndicated radio broadcast show hosted by Michael Baisden as a resident clairvoyant / insight advisor. Dorothea has appeared on a host of television shows including *Good Morning Peachtree* and *Peachtree in the Morning* in Atlanta, Georgia. Dorothea's motto is "Insight is the name of the game, and change is the goal. Hence, insight without change is meaningless."

Dorothea does a weekly Blog Talk Radio show. This show is to provide insight on the emotional roller coaster of events happening in your life. It's your platform to receive answers to questions you've been pondering or needing clarity too. Dorothea's Blog Talk Show, *Insight without Change Is Meaningless*, has been a weekly staple on Tuesdays at 9:00 p.m. for eight years. (Telephone or Skype this number: 323-580-5745.)

This is a show that will allow you to hear you're not alone in your dilemma because other people have similar difficulties, so through participating or listening, you can get clarity. There are no stupid or risqué questions. Ask anything that concerns you. This is an all-inclusive show, and everyone is welcome. This show is for the people. Whatever your lifestyle is or sexual orientation or religious and spiritual beliefs are, you are welcome. The purpose of this show is to pull you out of your complacency and get you to where you want to be. You may ask what clairvoyance is, and it is the ability to perceive matters beyond the range of ordinary perception—beyond the five senses. Now, with meditation daily twice a day, you can begin to come into alignment with your purpose and start having a stress-free life.

Life is full of twists and turns, and it is difficult at times to navigate smoothly in the direction you want to go toward. You ask and wonder why life isn't giving you what you ask for. Sometimes it's not the question that delays the outcome we want. It could be the emotion behind the question and the pent-up frustration that is keeping the answer from manifesting.

We are living in a world of daily changes, and every day and year, we have to be adaptable to those changes and at the same time not get caught up in the appearances of the next best thing. How to stay centered and grounded is the question.